Understanding the Euro

Foreword by Kenneth Clarke

Edited by Andrew Duff

FEDERAL TRUST

THE FEDERAL TRUST

The Federal Trust works through research and education towards the widening and deepening of the European Union as well as to enhance the European policy of the United Kingdom

The Trust conducts enquiries, promotes seminars and conferences and publishes reports and teaching materials on the European dimension.

Its current and future work programme includes studies of economic and monetary union, long-term change, civic education and the future of the European Parliament. Up-to-date information about the Federal Trust can be found on the internet at www.fedtrust.co.uk.

The Trust is the UK member of TEPSA (the Trans-European Policy Studies Association).

The Federal Trust is a registered charity and expresses no political view of its own.

The Trust's most recent publications are Yao-Su Hu and Donald Maitland, *Europe and Emerging Asia*, 1998; Ian Davidson, *Jobs and the Rhineland Model*, 1998; and Andrew Duff (ed.), *The Treaty of Amsterdam: Text and Commentary*, 1997.

Published by the Federal Trust
Dean Bradley House
52 Horseferry Road
London SW1P 2AF
© Federal Trust for Education and Research 1998
ISBN 0 901573 72 8
The Federal Trust is a Registered Charity
Marketing and Distribution by Kogan Page Ltd
Printed in the European Union

UNDERSTANDING THE EURO

Contents

Preface

The Federal Trust has been contributing to the debate about European economic and monetary union for over thirty years.

In 1972 it published an influential study group report, *European Monetary Integration*, by Giovanni Magnifico and John Williamson, in which the idea of a parallel currency, the 'Europa', was advanced as a way to move forward after the collapse of the Werner Plan. Since then we have continued to monitor progress, promote studies, make policy proposals and organise debate.

Today, after much controversy and with some trepidation, the European Union stands on the brink of the introduction of its single currency, the euro. The need for continual and critical assessment of EMU has never been stronger, especially in Britain, which, more nervous than others and in some ways different, stands aside from the project.

In such circumstances, the role of the Federal Trust is clear: to advance understanding of the single currency, especially within the United Kingdom.

This collection of essays seeks to answer some serious questions about the euro and sterling's participation in it. The authors were chosen because they are all well-informed about EMU. Some of us are what the newspapers call 'pro-Europeans'. But the authors were asked to be sceptical and not to duck the difficult issues, and were invited to be frank and bold in their treatment of them. They have been so, and I am most grateful to them all, and to Kenneth Clarke for his important foreword. Harry Cowie, Simon Nuttall and Anthony Teasdale also helped me with the book.

Articles of the Treaty are designated in old style and, in bold, in new style.

The Federal Trust welcomes comments on its publications. They should be addressed to me at the Federal Trust, Dean Bradley House, 52 Horseferry Road, London SW1P 2AF.

Andrew Duff

Director

September 1998

About the Authors

The Rt Hon. Kenneth Clarke QC MP was Chancellor of the Exchequer from May 1993 to May 1997.

David Begg is Professor of Economics at Birkbeck College in the University of London.

Alison Cottrell is Chief International Economist at Paine Webber International.

Iain Begg is Professor of International Economics at South Bank University, London.

Graham Bishop is European Adviser to Salomon Smith Barney.

John Monks has been General Secretary of the Trades Union Congress since 1993.

Lord Currie of Marylebone is Professor of Economics at the London Business School.

Christopher Johnson has been UK Adviser to the Association for the Monetary Union of Europe since 1991.

Peter Riddell is political columnist and commentator of The Times.

Peter Kellner is political commentator for the London Evening Standard, and election analyst for BBC Television.

Nigel Forman was a member of the Treasury Select Committee of the House of Commons, 1993-97.

John Stevens MEP has been a member of the Monetary Affairs Sub-Committee of the European Parliament since 1994.

Andrew Duff has been Director of the Federal Trust since 1993.

Glossary

CBI	Confederation of British Industry
Coreper	EU Committee of Permanent Representatives
DDR	German Democratic Republic
DTI	UK Department of Trade and Industry
ECB	European Central Bank
Ecofin	Council of economic and finance ministers
EMU	Economic and Monetary Union
ESCB	European System of Central Banks
EIB	European Investment Bank
ERM	Exchange Rate Mechanism
FDI	Foreign Direct Investment
G7	Group of Seven
GDP	Gross Domestic Product
GNP	Gross National Product
IGC	Intergovernmental Conference
IMF	International Monetary Fund
OECD	Organisation of Economic Cooperation & Development
QMV	Qualified Majority Vote
TENs	Trans-European Networks
TUC	Trades Union Congress
WTO	World Trade Organisation

A Chronology of EMU

1958	Monetary Committee established under the terms of the Treaty of Rome
1964	Committee of Central Bank Governors created to reduce potential for conflict between the six member states
1968	Completion of customs union
December 1969	Summit meeting at The Hague appoints Pierre Werner to report on how to reduce exchange rate volatility
March 1971	Council adopts Werner's three stage plan for EMU based on managing exchange rate fluctuations within a 'snake', a European Monetary Cooperation Fund, and the liberalisation of capital
August 1971	Dollar-based international Bretton Woods system collapses; finally abandoned in 1973
October 1972	Summit meeting in Paris confirms the goal of EMU by 1980
October 1973	Middle East war leads to oil supply crisis and financial turbulence: Werner Plan scuppered
October 1977	Roy Jenkins re-launches idea of monetary union
March 1979	European Monetary System created: small fluctuations around the European Currency Unit allowed within an Exchange Rate Mechanism, agreed jointly
March 1983	François Mitterrand adopts hard currency approach to stabilise franc against the DM
June 1983	Stuttgart European Council reaffirms commitment to European Union
June 1985	Commission launches ambitious programme to create the single market by the end of 1992
February 1986	Single European Act signed, strengthening coordination of economic policy

June 1988	At European Council in Hanover Helmut Kohl accepts need for integration of monetary and economic policy; study of EMU commissioned from Jacques Delors
July 1988	Liberalisation of capital movements
June 1989	European Council in Madrid accepts Delors report on EMU
February 1992	Treaty on European Union signed at Maastricht: three phase approach to EMU enshrined, involving tough convergence criteria
September 1992	UK and Italy forced to withdraw from ERM
August 1993	ERM band widened
December 1993	Commission White Paper on Growth, Competitiveness and Employment
January 1994	Stage Two of EMU begins; establishment of European Monetary Institute
December 1995	Madrid European Council decides on the name 'euro' and adopts changeover programme
January 1997	In the absence of a majority of member states meeting the convergence criteria, passage to Stage Three postponed
May 1998	Brussels European Council decides that 11 member states should go forward to Stage Three
July 1998	European Central Bank takes over from EMI
January 1999	Euro to be created. ESCB will take over responsibility for single monetary policy, foreign exchange operations and the TARGET payment system.
January 2002	Euro to appear in notes and coins
July 2002	National currencies will cease to have legal tender

Foreword

Kenneth Clarke

THE IMPORTANCE OF EMU

The European Union is poised to embark on the most ambitious and important initiative of its forty-year history. Next January, eleven EU member states will establish a continent-wide economic and monetary union, with a single currency and a common monetary policy. Less than ten years after the Madrid European Council of June 1989, which accepted the Delors Report on EMU and launched stage one of the process, the 'cloud cuckoo land' which Margaret Thatcher derided as politically impossible will be a working reality for several of the world's richest economies.

From day one, the effects of EMU will be significant. First, a single interest rate will be set for the whole single-currency area by a new, independent European Central Bank. That bank will operate by majority voting among the governors of the participating central banks and the other directors recently appointed to its board. It will have price stability as its overriding goal. Second, again from the very start, a new pan-European currency, the euro, will become the official currency of the eleven EMU states. Admittedly, for the first three years of EMU (1999-2001), existing national currencies remain as sub-divisions of the euro, interchangeable with it and with each other at fixed parities, on an entirely fungible basis. But the euro will be usable, and will be increasingly used, for commercial or official transactions that do not require cash. Then, in January 2002, euro notes and coins will be issued in their own right, paralleling national currencies for six months before replacing them forever. Less than four years from now, the franc, the mark, the guilder, and at least eight other national currencies, will be history. Europe will be in people's pockets as never before.

The longer-term effects of EMU promise to be no less dramatic. From its inception, the new euro-zone will encompass 300 million consumers. It will be the second largest, single-currency economic area in the world, representing almost as big a share of global GDP and international trade as the United States. Within this huge economy, the pooling of monetary sovereignty should promote less volatile interest rates. The absolute commitment to price stability should cement low inflation in perpetuity. The fiscal framework — the 3% budget deficit ceiling, bolstered by the Stability and Growth Pact — will help institutionalise sound finances and small 'c' conservative economics on a continental scale. EMU will give a huge and powerful boost to orthodox economic management and financial stability at the heart of the European and world economies.

Internationally the euro is likely to emerge quickly as a genuinely global currency, challenging the dollar as a serious alternative for traders and investors worldwide. The appeal of the euro, the cautiously-managed currency of a very large trading bloc, will lie in the stability it offers as a reserve currency and as a denominator of commodities and trade. In the process, Europe's influence in international economic decision-making will be greatly enhanced. In September 1992, when France was debating the Maastricht Treaty, President Mitterrand was asked about the significance of its EMU chapter. His reply was simple: the single currency had the potential to make Europe an economic superpower. He was right.

In the domestic economy, the long-term, supply-side dynamic of EMU promises to be equally radical. The use of one currency will mean full transparency of investment and pricing in a 300-million consumer zone. The creation of a single European capital market, with access to a single pool of savings, will be greatly advanced. Cross-border investment and trade will grow. A super league of European multinationals, freed from the constraints of national stock markets, will steadily emerge. A massive process of rationalisation is about to be unleashed, first in banking and financial services, then across the economy as a whole. The combination of one money and one market is set to offer greater choice and lower prices to consumers Europe-wide.

EMU will be a powerful agent promoting a supply-side revolution across Europe. Already much-needed structural reforms — through deregulation, privatisation, better value for money in state spending and greater labour-market flexibility — have been greatly encouraged by the race to get public finances in order to qualify for EMU entry. This process will continue and is likely to become a way of life once the single currency is up and running. And by making the European economy more efficient by removing exchange-rate uncertainties and transaction costs, and allowing transparency of pricing in the euro-zone, the single currency will create a competitive climate even more intense than the single market. Governments have not only had to liberalise the economy to get in and stay in EMU, they will want to continue doing so to remain competitive within the world's largest single-currency single market. The liberalising, free-market logic of EMU is overwhelming.

Euro-fact and fiction

Critics of EMU, claim that, whatever the economic advantages, the single currency will over time centralise economic policy, significantly boost European-level spending, require European-level taxation, and as a result of all three greatly stimulate the development of some kind of European state. These assertions are, I believe, wrong. Certainly, by definition, EMU does and must involve the merging of monetary sovereignty, with an independent central bank setting one interest rate and controlling the supply of a single currency across the participating countries. The key question is: does a single monetary policy require and lead to a European economic government, with central control over taxation and spending?

The Maastricht Treaty at least is quite clear on this point. The EMU design does not envisage the transfer of economic sovereignty in any way, bar one. There will be binding limits on budget deficits, to prevent any country running up debts which it could finance at a lower interest rate than if it were outside the euro-zone. Within that borrowing limit, countries will remain free to set the level and composition of their taxation and spending. Competitive forces are likely to keep taxes and spending lower overall than they might otherwise be, but states will remain free to choose a high-tax, high-spend mix if they wish, even if the more probable result will be a somewhat lower tax and spend take than at present. The single market already builds pressure in this lower tax and spend direction; the single currency will enhance it. The one option ruled out is a combination of high spend and low tax. In this respect, EMU is the institutionalisation of economic virtue.

Will there be a central, coordinated macro-economic policy in Europe? Naturally, as at present and indeed for many years past, member states will regard general economic policy as a matter of common concern. Properly converged, they are likely to run at broadly the same point in the cycle, something which is already the case in the Deutschmark zone. Beyond that, there can and will be no fiscal fine-tuning from the centre, because the EU budget is very small (1.27% of GDP) and legally cannot run in deficit. It is almost certain to stay that way. A majority of member states are now net contributors. There is no serious market for greater EU spending. Nothing remotely on the cards envisages endowing the European Commission or the Ecofin Council with the economic instruments of a state.

Will taxes need to be levied at European level? Without higher EU spending, obviously not. Will there be greater harmonisation of national taxes to underpin transparency of pricing? To a limited degree, perhaps. There is already a measure of harmonisation of rates and form of certain consumer taxes: the last Conservative government in Britain agreed to the installation of a minimum standard rate of VAT across the EU. But tax harmonisation measures require unanimous agreement among the member states, and any change in that position would itself require unanimous approval. In the 1996-97 Intergovernmental Conference the idea of majority voting for taxation proved a complete non-starter. The idea that under EMU tax powers will be transferred to Europe is simply untrue. Except on monetary policy and excessive deficits, countries within EMU will stay separate decision-making entities, able to choose domestic economic policies which the international financial markets will bear.

Failure of nerve

Where does all this leave Britain, which falls comfortably within the formal convergence criteria of the Maastricht Treaty (on debt, deficits, inflation and long-term interest rates), but negotiated an opt-out from EMU which we have chosen to invoke for 1999? In a welcome development, the new Labour government declared last autumn that it had no objection in principle to EMU entry. It said, quite sensibly, that it saw no constitutional bar to UK membership and would judge the issue solely on whether the economic conditions were right. Tony Blair even went so far as to say that he wanted Britain to be a member of a successful single currency, a view which I myself firmly share.

However, in a statement to the House of Commons which he may yet come to regret, Chancellor Gordon Brown also announced that the government did not wish or expect Britain to participate in EMU during the lifetime of the current parliament, which theoretically could run until June 2002, and that we would only enter if and when certain 'British economic tests' had been achieved. The Chancellor spoke of there being 'no realistic prospect of our having demonstrated before the end of this Parliament that we have achieved convergence that is sustainable and settled, rather than transitory ...'. He went on: 'Therefore, barring some fundamental or unforeseen change in economic circumstances, making a decision to join during this Parliament is not realistic'.

I myself have never taken the view that Britain should join EMU at the start in January 1999, and few people ever have. But many, including myself, have been equally opposed to ruling out UK entry on any inflexible timetable beyond that date. There is certainly no reason why we should now necessarily exclude the possibility of membership very early in the next century, most notably in January 2002, when euro notes and coins begin to circulate. Strictly speaking, the government has not done that. But Gordon Brown came perilously close to foreclosing such an option by the language he used in announcing his EMU policy. It represented, I fear, not the confident assertion of a popular government with a large majority, and at least four and a half years ahead of it, but the voice of a strangely intimidated government afraid to use its position of strength to assert controversial positions in the national interest. It is difficult to escape the view that, in its handling of the EMU issue at a critical time, the Blair government suffered something of a failure of nerve, and one which may have serious long-term consequences.

My own fear, and that of many others, is that the longer the UK stays outside EMU, the bigger the disadvantages of non-membership may become, and also the more difficult we may find it actually to get in. Outside the euro-zone, the pound could well be very unstable. Creating the world's second largest currency overnight in the middle of our largest trading market is bound to put particular strain on sterling. The competing gravitational pulls of the dollar and euro could leave the pound like a ping-pong ball between two footballs, moving around even more spectacularly than it has since 1992. Exchange-rate instability will be a problem in itself for the UK economy, potentially making convergence more difficult, but it would be compounded if any attempt were made to insist on prior membership of the new, post-1999 exchange rate mechanism (ERM2) of the European Monetary System.

Outside EMU, the UK is likely to lose a good deal of its attractiveness as the European Union's premier centre for inward investment from third countries. It will also be a less obvious location for inward investment from within the EU itself. Once the continental single market has its own single currency, the achievements of the last two decades in converting Britain into what the last government liked to style the 'enterprise centre of Europe' may become much less important in attracting foreign investment. Continental economies of scale could increasingly dwarf any supply-side comparative advantages enjoyed by the UK. To capitalise on those advantages, business will probably see UK membership of EMU as increasingly necessary.

A further key problem for Britain outside EMU will be our declining leverage on the economic environment in which we operate. We are likely gradually to lose a great deal of our political influence in European economic decision-making. A Europe-wide interest rate will be set without any British in-put. A committee of the eleven EMU member state finance ministers will be caucusing before each Ecofin Council meeting to pre-settle the key agenda items. Pressure will develop for G7 meetings to shake down into a G3 format, with Britain's place at the top table seriously at risk.

Cyclical convergence

So, faced with this difficult prospect, when should the UK contemplate joining the single European currency? The decision not to enter in 1999 is clearly the right one. After seven years of economic growth, we are further advanced in the economic cycle than most of our continental partners, and our short-term interest rates diverge from those of the future euro-zone. It certainly makes sense to hold off until a more convergent pattern of performance between Britain and the EMU Eleven has been attained. A greater degree of cyclical convergence — not one of the formal criteria perhaps, but a sensible practical indicator nonetheless — does need to be achieved before entry.

Although the single market has done much to integrate Europe's economies and erode structural differences, ultimately this question of cyclical synchronisation is something of a chicken and egg problem. One reason why the founding members of EMU have been able successfully to align their economies is precisely because the markets believed they would be founder members of EMU. The spectacular convergence of first long-term and then short-term interest rates on the continent is testimony to that. As yield differentials disappeared, one leading German banker put it neatly last year: 'EMU already exists, without the euro'.

It follows that if Britain signals its firm intention to join within a given time-frame, UK interest rates are just as likely as Italy's or Spain's have already been to converge on those of the core states. Cyclical factors mean that over the next couple of years, continental rates will probably rise and, one hopes, UK rates will fall in the natural order of things. Policy should be designed to ensure that, as the British economy slows and the euro-zone expands, our interest rates align like tram lines coming together — rather than head off in different directions, like ships passing in the night. A heavy burden falls upon the government to ensure that this critical opportunity to position Britain as a credible EMU pre-in is not missed or squandered.

Once a greater degree of cyclical convergence has occurred, there is little else that needs to be done before the UK can enter EMU. The structural fundamentals are good. We enjoy a high level of flexibility in both labour and product markets. We have a strong record on liberalisation, deregulation and privatisation. The economy is now much more capable than in the past of sustaining non-inflationary growth. Every silver lining has a cloud, but the biggest cloud, the exchange-rate instability of sterling, is itself in part a product of uncertainty about our intentions towards monetary union.

The government does cite proper synchronisation as one of its various 'British economic tests'. However, holding off for perfect synchronisation to be attained could all too easily slip into rolling postponement until a long list of optimal conditions prevail. Too many of the government's unilateral membership tests are subjective, tautological or platitudinous. Nobody will recommend entry if, for example, they think EMU would be bad for business or investment or growth or jobs or the City. Yet these are cited as objective yardsticks. The government talks repeatedly of needing a 'period of stability ... to ensure that convergence [is] sustainable and durable'. How long does this period of stability need to last? We are never told, except mysteriously that it extends until after the next general election.

Getting to go

The big risk in the British government's current approach to EMU is that it underestimates the serious difficulties which may cloud its room for manoeuvre at home in respect of UK entry say four, five or six or years from now. Will the government be as popular in the next parliament as in this one? Will there be as big a pro-EMU majority in the House of Commons? Will the domestic economy be doing as well? However much public support there may be for EMU at some future date, there is no guarantee that an unpopular government could actually win the vote. And if Labour is not confident enough now, with so much going for it, to risk a referendum in this parliament, will it be sufficiently confident, when the time comes, to risk one in the next? There are legitimate reasons for doubt.

In the interim, the government has decided to hack EMU into the long grass. In the process, quite unnecessarily, it has chosen to tie its own hands, mainly through fear of the media reaction to any early commitment to join. Fighting and winning a referendum is a problem it would prefer to defer. It assumes that business preparations will develop an unstoppable momentum of their own, which will carry public opinion before it. Instead of leading opinion, the government hopes to be able to follow it, minimising political risks to its popularity and prospects of reelection.

Even if British public opinion is gradually becoming more positive towards EMU, it is unlikely to shift decisively unless the government is prepared to take risks and put some of its still considerable political capital on the line. A big majority in parliament and a strong economy give it a much better backdrop to lead on EMU than ever the Heath government enjoyed, for example, in taking Britain into the EC in 1973.

Postponing any serious discussion of British entry beyond the next election, as the Blair government is trying to do, is neither good for Britain nor good for the integrity of the euro-system. We need to be able to take the decision at the right time, not when it happens to be politically convenient to the government. There will always be danger in seeking a mandate to join: that's the nature of democratic politics. The option of a risk-free referendum on EMU simply does not exist, however long we wait.

In getting the right glide-path to British membership, our continental partners also have an important role to play. The leading players in the new euro-zone need to be encouraged to respond to the UK's commitment in principle to join by aiming to make life easier, not more difficult, for the advocates of EMU entry in Britain. Evidence of deliberate and gratuitous exclusion from key deliberations of the new Euro Eleven committee, for example, could play badly with UK public opinion. Equally, any attempt to insist on a formal two-year membership of the new ERM2 would make British entry into EMU more problematic. We can all agree on the importance of demonstrable currency stability, but having to rejoin an exchange-rate system is not the most sensible means of demonstrating it. The carefully-crafted wording on the ERM in the Council decision this May codifying Sweden's refusal to join EMU in 2002 is an encouraging signal of possible flexibility on this front. The best way to induce the right response from our partners is to make it clear to them that our intentions about joining are serious.

To regain the initiative at home and abroad, and prepare the British public and business for EMU entry, the government needs to revisit its position on the single currency. It should announce sooner rather than later that, assuming the economics work out as we expect, Britain intends to join EMU early in the next decade, either in 2002 or 2003. The government could then call a referendum at a time of its choosing, either in this parliament or the next, to get a public mandate for membership on that basis. The electorate needs to be given the early prospect of making a choice about EMU so that, if we are to join, we can make a success of our preparations as a nation for membership of the euro-zone.

The euro matters to Britain and Europe. In or out of EMU, the single currency will shape this country's place in the European Union and the world for decades to come. It is therefore a great pleasure to have been invited to introduce a serious book about monetary union. Andrew Duff has brought together a series of respected commentators from a variety of backgrounds who aim to do two things: they offer an intelligent and accessible assessment of the implications of EMU, and they confront directly the criticisms made by EMU's opponents of its political acceptability and economic sustainability. This book is to be warmly recommended as a major contribution to the most important political and economic debate of our time.

1. Is EMU an Ambush?

David Begg

The first attempt to create an economic and monetary union among the member states of the European Community foundered in the 1970s. In June 1983 the European Council at Stuttgart sought to revive the integration process by confirming their commitment to 'ever closer union' and by setting out on a new road to forge a single market. This strategy for a fresh start for European unification was signed up to by all the heads of state or government, including Mrs Thatcher; presumably she thought the complete venture sufficiently distant and improbable that she preferred to conserve her ammunition for more immediate skirmishes. Yet the single market has been largely accomplished, and the single currency will begin within eleven member states in January 1999. Even though the UK will not be in the first wave of members, many British firms are already making plans to quote prices in euros and well as in pounds.

In part the Stuttgart Declaration reflected the bicycle theory of integration: when riders are inexperienced, any interruption to forward momentum is likely to cause a nasty accident. The sequencing of challenges was therefore chosen with care. First, the single market, anticipated to be a project with identifiable economic benefits, substantially more winners than losers, and hence likely to be economically successful and popular politically. Public enthusiasm thus kindled, the next easiest project would be attempted. If a single currency could be made to work, yet more difficult challenges could be confronted: moving towards a single budget and eventually to political integration itself.

The question I wish to pose is whether the adoption of the euro is likely to require rapid progress towards much closer fiscal integration, either by more explicit harmonisation and coordination of national budget policies or by actual transfer of greater budgetary powers to Brussels. If monetary integration requires fiscal integration to make it work, any attempt to portray EMU as the terminus of the process of European integration will be simply a fiscal ambush. EMU members may subsequently find that they are prepared to cede fiscal sovereignty rather than admit defeat of the single currency. Foreseeing this, more judicious countries should regard membership of the single currency as a choice between federalism and national sovereignty.

This contention deserves careful scrutiny but it is important not to be intellectually careless. Guilt by association is not a reliable standard of proof. A more rigorous examination must consider how much monetary sovereignty is sacrificed by joining EMU, and what that additional sovereignty could accomplish, even if used wisely. Nor can the evolution of Western Europe be attributed solely to monetary decisions made during the late 1990s. Indeed, the converse is more likely: it is because other forces have been so powerful that money is finally being integrated too. Any reliable assessment of the danger of a fiscal ambush caused by EMU must accurately distinguish fiscal pressures to which EMU will give rise from fiscal pressures that would anyway have been experienced. If these latter forces are sufficiently great, the fiscal ambush exists independently of whether a country joins the single currency or not. Let me begin by indicating what these forces are.

Fiscal sovereignty is being steadily undermined anyway

In the design of economic policy, national sovereignty exists only to the extent that the relevant goods, services, capital and people are relatively immobile across national frontiers. When the fortress walls are high enough, those inside can make choices without regard to the outside world. High economic walls may be constructed by nature (transport costs, physical distance), by custom and culture (language, familiarity, taste), or by government (tariffs, regulations, home bias in procurement and hiring).

When the walls are lower, more interactions take place with other countries: trade in goods and services, labour migration, flows of capital. If the walls are very low, cross-border flows become very easy, and therefore very sensitive to special treatment in one country but not another. A single country, acting unilaterally, may now find that taxation quickly leads to an outflow of the thing being taxed, perhaps to such an extent that, foreseeing this, the national government prefers not to raise the tax rate in the first place. Similarly, subsidies of domestic activities may induce inflows from abroad to take advantage of these subsidies; again, a government may be deterred from pursuing a policy that otherwise it would have wished to adopt. Ease of cross-border flows thus erodes national sovereignty.

Nobody would seriously suggest that the City of Westminster and the London Borough of Camden have different interest rates. Mobility of money between the two is so high that any systematic and persisting interest differential would induce a tidal wave of money from one to the other. Westminster and Camden do not have distinct monetary sovereignty. Goods and people move less easily than money, but substantially differing tax rates in Westminster and Camden (more precisely, substantially differing tax rates not offset by the implicit local services simultaneously provided) would also induce flows to such an extent that fiscal sovereignty is diminished, though not entirely eliminated.

In the same way, the Chancellor of the Exchequer cannot levy the tax rate on cans of beer that the Treasury would otherwise wish to impose. Already, around 10% of beer cans drunk in UK households are purchased by those households in France. Higher UK excise duty, unmatched by a rise in French duty, might so diminish UK beer can sales that revenue to the UK Treasury might fall. The unambiguous winner in such an exercise would be the French Treasury, whose tax receipts would rise if *British* tax rates increased. The same point applies to the welfare state. Any country wishing unilaterally to be generous is likely to attract both legal and illegal immigrants; fear of such induced immigration may then inhibit generosity of national policy makers.

These examples make clear that sovereignty has two dimensions, the ease with which cross-border flows occur and the extent of altruism citizens of one jurisdiction feel towards those in another. When high rates of property tax in London drive businesses to the provinces, Londoners may feel sufficient altruism for fellow Brits to impute some of the benefits, and thus may not be deterred from setting high tax rates in the first place. The same consideration applies to all forms of redistribution.

Viewed through these spectacles, European integration is a process being driven largely by technological progress. Transport costs are coming down, making distribution to neighbouring countries easier; satellites are no respecters of national boundaries; foreign travel is increasing familiarity with foreign customs. It is legitimate to ask which of these processes are European and which truly global. The internet is geographically blind, but familiarity and cultural similarity is more localised; transport costs, though lower, are still high enough to favour near rather than distant markets; and the economic gains from integration of a collection of small contiguous countries continues to outweigh the economic gains from closer integration with larger and distant countries, with whom relatively free international trade remains, for now, the best practical alternative.

Pressure for closer European integration is therefore more than the fruit of cultural ambition or the ultimate realisation of a postwar European peace dividend; it is the product of continuing economic development that is realigning the configuration of the relevant economic jurisdiction over which policy should sensibly be made. Of course, it is happening slowly and irregularly, but it continues to take place and is unlikely to be halted, let alone reversed. The question is not whether European policy should become more integrated, but in what dimensions and at what rate.

To sum up so far, fiscal sovereignty has already been partly eroded by forces increasing mobility within Europe, accelerated by the single market programme designed to diminish man-made impediments to cross-border flows. Greater competition in markets for products, for capital and for labour have resulted in fiscal competition in the unilateral actions of nation states, exerting pressure for lower tax rates (to attract or import tax bases for abroad) and for lower welfare spending (either to export neediness abroad or at least to prevent its further import).

As European integration increases, the attempt to preserve national sovereignty will therefore be a recipe for a declining role for the state. As such, one should expect such a policy to be favoured by those who believe anyway that small government is good government. Conversely, any serious attempt to sustain higher taxes and higher welfare spending is likely to founder unless it can be coordinated throughout the region within which goods, people and capital are mobile; only then do the highly taxed have nowhere to which to escape and only then can generous welfare be provided without importing further welfare dependants.

This diagnosis suggests that completion of a single European market, to which all EU countries are already committed, may already amount to a Trojan horse for greater fiscal integration. If increasing fiscal competition in the unilateral actions of nation states drives the role of the state below some threshold of efficiency or fairness, the only coherent response will be to open negotiations for greater fiscal integration within the EU. Indeed, many ad hoc instances of such negotiations can already be observed. Of course, the need for greater centralisation of some activities can be combined with a determination to maintain decentralised diversity where possible, as affirmed by the principle of subsidiarity.

Would remaining outside EMU slow this process down? Only if it inhibited creation of the single market itself. Exactly how much the single currency will boost the single market remains unclear — serious empirical research has found it difficult to identify large gains from moving from reasonably fixed to completely fixed exchange rates — but fortunately it is unnecessary to take a stand on this issue. The eleven first wave EMU members will already constitute a critical mass likely to achieve whatever gains in continental European competition are to be had from the single market cum single currency. Once German pension funds and insurance companies are no longer constrained to hold assets denominated only in DM, but can now access the entire EMU area and in consequence develop a much wider horizon, British pension funds and insurance companies will become increasingly aware of the foreign competition regardless of whether the UK joins EMU or not.

In this section, I have argued that the UK's fiscal sovereignty has already been partly eroded, and that this will continue as part of the wider forces of integration which the UK long ago accepted: all political parties in the UK profess enthusiasm for the single market in Europe. Yet further completion of the single market, as a result both of technical advances and policy decisions, is likely at some point to create a powerful case for greater fiscal cooperation whether or not member states have a single currency. Remaining outside EMU is unlikely to prevent this occurring.

I turn next to the additional fiscal pressures that are the direct consequence of a decision to participate in EMU.

What monetary sovereignty is for

Since prices are denominated in money values, control of the money supply eventually determines the price level; once all market forces have worked themselves out, a lower money supply implies a lower price level. About this there is no dispute, though economists continue to argue about issues finessed by the careful wording of the previous sentence. Who decides what the level of the money stock will be: is it chosen by the monetary authority or is it determined passively to accommodate the budget financing needs of the fiscal authority? And what is the duration of the period necessary for market forces to work themselves out, restoring the economy to full capacity whatever the level of money and prices?

Unless all markets, not just for financial instruments but also for goods and especially labour, adjust extremely quickly, an economy will not operate continuously at full capacity merely by the operation of market forces alone. Policy intervention then might help but might not: since it takes time to diagnose a problem and implement a new course for policy, and further time to affect private behaviour, well-meaning policy intervention may boost the economy just at the time market forces, unassisted, have finally eliminated a recession. Of course, the more sluggish the economy, the less scope there is for well-intended policy intervention to mess things up.

Nor is there much disagreement about the relative sluggishness of different economies: continental Europe is more sluggish than the UK, which is more sluggish than the USA. Thus, US business cycles should be less protracted, but, precisely for that reason, US policy makers need to be more nimble if they are to improve upon the market outcome. Taking years to get a tax cut through a gridlocked Congress is insufficiently nimble for this purpose.

Two types of policy offer greater hope: the first is automatic stabilisers, policies that dampen the cycle without requiring any discretionary action. Examples include income tax and unemployment benefit. At given tax and benefit rates, tax revenues increase and unemployment payments diminish in a boom, both serving to damp down the cycle. Of course, automatic stabilisers are less effective when (marginal) tax rates are low and benefit levels ungenerous. A single European market, coupled with uncoordinated national fiscal policy making, is thus a recipe for increasingly less assistance from automatic stabilisers.

This leaves, second, monetary policy. Interest rates can be adjusted rapidly, and, in a small open economy like the UK, this not merely impacts slowly on domestic spending but also has an immediate impact on the exchange rate and competitiveness.

Previously, I argued that cross-border fiscal spillovers were on the increase. In some areas, such as taxation of capital and of alcohol, such spillovers are already large. In other areas, such as taxation of labour, fiscal spillovers are still quite small; labour mobility is not yet that large. Whatever the level of fiscal spillovers, monetary spillovers are an order of magnitude larger. Financial capital is extremely mobile, and in consequence monetary sovereignty is already quite low, whatever the monetary policy in force.

Let me give two examples in relation to the UK: first, Black Wednesday; second, the dilemma of the Bank of England's Monetary

Policy Committee during the first year of its existence. Any UK interest rates high enough to stop the UK economy overheating will, given the low level of foreign interest rates, induce a sharp sterling appreciation and make UK exports very uncompetitive. Hence, the UK financial media still pays just as much attention to US and continental European interest rates as it used to when the UK was formally inside the Exchange Rate Mechanism.

Countries that are very interdependent should consider cooperation precisely to stop inflicting large spillovers on one another; that, rather than a reduction in transaction costs or exchange rate uncertainty, is the best case for EMU. Trade within Europe is now so integrated that multilateral interest rate disarmament makes sense. The UK, an offshore island with a global past, is a little less integrated than most continental countries, but this is only a matter of degree; European trade is much the most significant share of UK trade, and that share continues to increase.

It is important now to take stock of what monetary policy can and cannot do. In the long run (once market forces have restored full capacity), monetary policy can *only* affect prices. Low inflation is desirable, and can be achieved either by appropriate domestic monetary policy or by participating in a monetary union that also pursues a sound monetary policy.

A monetary expansion (lower interest rates) can give the economy a temporary boost but, in time, higher wages and other market forces will undo this effect. Similarly, and crucially, depreciation of the exchange rate can only have temporary effects on output: the boom induced gradually bids up domestic wages and prices, eliminating the initial increase in competitiveness.

Giving up the ability to devalue the exchange rate does not mean giving up the ability to boost the economy in the long run. Neither the exchange rate nor any other aspect of monetary policy had this power in the first place. Neither southern Italy nor southern Spain could ever have solved their high unemployment problem by seceding and devaluing their new currencies. Long-term structural problems need structural solutions.

In practice, to unlock the gains from interest rate disarmament, from lower transactions costs, and from elimination of exchange rate uncertainty, a country joining EMU has to pay one significant price: it has to give up the unilateral ability to use domestic interest rates, and the consequent exchange rate, to dampen its domestic business cycle. How great a price is this?

As I observed above, even for a country outside the single currency, the central bank may be reluctant to use interest rates vigorously for that purpose: since it can control neither domestic fiscal policy nor foreign interest rates, it may dislike the exchange rate consequences of the interest rate policy that would be required to counteract the overheating effects of domestic fiscal policy. Whatever the difficulties entailed by EMU, one should not make the mistake of supposing that the alternative always works well.

Consequences of EMU membership

Economies get blown away from full capacity both by shocks that affect demand and by shocks that affect supply and full capacity itself. Either way, economies that are sluggish in adjustment return only slowly to full capacity.

Suppose the UK joined EMU. It would experience two kinds of shocks, those shared by other EMU countries and those specific to the UK. In the former case, with all EMU countries suffering together (whether from recession or from overheating), the constraint of having a single monetary policy would not itself be a constraint at all: the change in monetary policy appropriate for one country would be appropriate for all. The potential problem is now narrowed down to the following circumstance: what would happen in the case of a country-specific shock that prompted no change in the euro interest rates since other members were unaffected?

How likely is such a problem? In the last decade, an army of empirical researchers has attempted to establish cross-country correlations of shocks, keeping track separately of demand shocks and supply shocks since they require different policy responses. This research has reached a fairly clear conclusion. There is an evident core of countries — the usual suspects — in which the correlation of shocks, although by no means perfect, is now quite high. These countries really are more integrated than the rest. Being more integrated, a single monetary policy will on many occasions suffice: Belgium rarely suffers a slump when France is booming. Outside the core is the periphery: Scandinavia, the UK, Ireland, and the Mediterranean fringe. They are less correlated with the others; for such countries, membership is more of a risk.

Before assessing whether that risk is containable, one health warning should be issued. Past correlations may quickly become a poor guide to future behaviour. EMU may itself cause industrial relocation in response to a better secured single market, and greater integration will increase cross-country correlations. Even more significantly, EMU will increase the correlation of macroeconomic policy across its member states by ending the possibility of pursuing divergent monetary policies.

Asymmetries are therefore likely to diminish, if only slowly. It would, however, be foolhardy to rely on instant and total integration to obviate the need for country-specific remedies by eliminating country-specific shocks. For individual member states of EMU, unable to use separate interest rates or exchange rates against their main trading partners, fiscal policy is the only remaining policy weapon with which to fight country-specific shocks.

This fiscal action can be conducted either at the federal EMU level or by national governments. One of the principal pieces of evidence often adduced in support of the contention that a fiscal federation will become inevitable is the fact that such a federation supports the largest existing monetary union, the USA. The existence of the federal tax system means that when California booms, 30 cents of each extra dollar of state income goes automatically to Washington via the federal income tax. In addition, 10 cents fewer is received from Washington because the welfare burden in California has fallen. Conversely, for each dollar by which income in Texas falls during a slump, Texans have to pay 30 cents less in federal taxes and receive 10 cents more in federal subsidies from Washington. Each US state appears to have 40% insurance of its state income, without any tax or subsidy rate being changed in Washington. If this is what quarantines Texas from pressure to devalue the Texas dollar during a Texas slump, surely Europe will be driven inexorably to put something similar in place? Hence the fiscal ambush.

In fact, this argument is much less powerful than it first appears. Suppose in 1999 a reduction in income in Texas induces transfers from Washington to the tune of 40% of the fall in Texas income. What happens in subsequent years? If the Texan slump was uncorrelated with performance in other US states, the federal budget will be affected little in the aggregate. However, if other states were also experiencing a slump, the federal budget will be affected much more severely and federal tax rates will have to increase in subsequent years.

In the latter case, there is no insurance value to be had from membership of a fiscal federation. A member state could instead have borrowed to fund deficit spending on its own national budget, thereby achieving the immediate fiscal boost to offset the slump and also incurring the subsequently higher tax liability to service a level of government debt that has risen correspondingly. Hence, the mutual insurance society works only when incomes in different member states are uncorrelated (or, even better, are negatively correlated).

So much for the argument in theory. What about the facts? First, the famous conclusion that US states are insured up to 40 cents in the dollar on fluctuations in state income is incorrect: the original studies failed to examine the correlation of fluctuations across states and hence the associated change in each state's future tax liability. Taking account of this, the true insurance that US states derive from the federal fiscal system is around 10 cents in the dollar, only one quarter of the original estimate. Insurance of 10% is not negligible, but nor is it indispensable.

Second, this figure may be even lower for EMU countries. The entire purpose of the famous Maastricht convergence criteria has been to make the structure of EMU members much more similar to one another than it was a decade ago. Increasing the correlation of the economies of member states makes a common monetary policy more appropriate, but it also diminishes opportunities for mutual insurance through a federal fiscal system. In so doing, it destroys one of the key arguments deployed by those contending that a fiscal ambush is an inevitable corollary of EMU.

Where country-specific shocks are not temporary changes in demand but permanent changes in supply there is ultimately no alternative to adjusting national output to the new level of national capacity. Reluctance to do so may give rise to pressures not for temporary transfers to smooth a cycle but for permanent transfers to subsidised regions that cannot or will not adjust. Systematic and sustained regional transfers already take place within countries and across the EU. Their extent partly reflects the political willingness to redistribute, even across national boundaries. Long run structural difficulties, however, cannot be solved by devaluation or other uses of monetary policy.

The advent of EMU therefore does nothing to create additional long term difficulties; nor does it provide any consequent stimulus to fiscal Europe. Indeed, paradoxically, the Maastricht restrictions now enshrined in the Stability Pact, whose purpose was to underpin sound money, has so focused attention on the evolution of debt and deficits that it may actually curtail transfers as a response to permanent supply shocks.

With regard to temporary demand shocks, if member states are to be able to use their national budgets as shock absorbers to smooth out temporary country-specific shocks to demand for their output, the Stability Pact must not get in the way. The intention of the Pact is to prevent medium term fiscal irresponsibility not to preclude short term actions that, being soon reversed, pose no longer term threat. The Pact can be redesigned to accomplish both roles simultaneously but at present the allowance it makes for temporary actions is rather rudimentary. Fixing the Pact, for example by more explicit reference to cyclically adjusted budget positions, will be much easier than inventing fiscal federalism in Europe.

2. Sustaining EMU

Alison Cottrell

'If you thought he was clear, you must have misunderstood'

Andrea Mitchell (Mrs Alan Greenspan), on her husband.

Central bankers and economists alike are renowned for obfuscation, so in an obviously painful departure from stereotype, let us be absolutely clear on one important point from the outset. It is entirely possible that EMU collapses. Failure is, indeed, an option; and the very last section of the population to rule it out would be an international investment community which, having witnessed German reunification, Yugoslavian disintegration, an ERM of ever-changing dimensions, and an Italian inflation rate of below 2%, has grown accustomed to a dozen 'impossible' things happening before breakfast.

It was only to be expected that a recent survey should find virtually no UK fund manager willing to voice absolute conviction in EMU surviving for five years (or in its not surviving for five years).[1] When asked for their opinion, two thirds of respondents ticked, predictably, the box representing a 'positive but more than 25%' chance of an EMU collapse; a result which says far less about the incidence of City of London Euro-scepticism, than about the natural reaction of investors asked about events half a decade away. Unsurprisingly, over half of those surveyed had no risk management programme in place to cope with EMU's collapse. Not being prepared to rule something out is not, after all, the same thing as expecting it to happen.

Fund managers blessed with absolute conviction are, fortunately, few and far between — and the sympathies of the majority of the population must go out to that minority whose pensions they manage. That EMU may not be sustainable is inarguable. To assert that it is unsustainable is, however, less a statement of fact than an expression of wish-fulfilment, and has implications going well beyond the mere (sic) collapse of a monetary system. If EMU folds, Europe's political structure implodes. It is difficult to see how the continental political mainstream could remain intact, or even recognisable, in the afterglow. Fortunately, an unhappy denouement is by no means as inevitable as it is depicted in some corners of the media; but this should not allow even the most single-minded Euro-proponent to rest on his or her laurels.

A sustainable EMU is not the same thing as a successful EMU; and neither equates to an EMU which is seen to have succeeded. A sustained but unsuccessful EMU would be the most miserable of all worlds, and while such a combination carries a low probability, it is not, unfortunately, a contradiction in terms.

Let us begin, however, with the issue of sustainability; or, as some might prefer, with EMU's unsustainability. If EMU falls to earth in a heap of feathers, this may be because some of its members have jumped out, or because they have been pushed; and it may have occurred acrimoniously, or with a modicum of goodwill. (A background of general chaos can be taken as a given.)

Jumping out of EMU

It is not too taxing to envisage the circumstances under which an EMU member might toy with 'jumping'. When European growth next slows, unemployment will once again ratchet up; in many cases, from an already high base.

An EMU-wide single monetary policy will never be appropriate for all local needs, any more than policy set in, for example, Threadneedle Street fits always and simultaneously the requirements of each sector and region in the UK economy. Differences in balance sheets, in wage and price behaviour, in psychology, in the transmission of central bank decisions to commercial bank rates, and in the very viability of banks and their customers in the newly competitive post-EMU environment; all of these will prevent any ECB decision having a uniform impact. This does not, of itself, constitute an argument against EMU; but that there will always be some regions and voters feeling disadvantaged by the common monetary policy is potentially more disruptive when the disgruntlement is directed towards a European Central Bank based physically in Frankfurt, than in a monetary union which coincides with the electoral boundaries of the nation state.

Fiscal flexibility should, of course, be able to act as a leveller, but if budget deficits have been run down aggressively in the good times, there may be little room left for fiscal expansion in the bad without Stability Pact constraints being hit. This is particularly true for highly indebted countries, given the likely need under such circumstances to divert an increasing proportion of spending to debt servicing. The probability of Stability Pact fines ever actually being levied is negligible.

However, the general confusion as to whether or not such action would or should be taken, and the inevitable accompanying disagreements between finance ministers and central bankers, would itself unnerve bond markets and push up relative long term interest rates, even if the ECB could somehow be persuaded to hold short term rates steady.

That greater intra-EMU transfers might be called upon to defuse the situation, is a possibility but only a very small one. The EU is, at heart, a legislative body, not a fiscally redistributive one, and there are no signs of any forthcoming fundamental shift in this regard. While greater fiscal coordination is certainly the road down which the euro Eleven are going, fiscal integration in the sense of expanding cross-EMU transfers appears extremely unlikely, especially given the new demands of EU enlargement.

Certainly, severe shocks to the EMU bloc could boost integration in many aspects of policy, and not just the economic. At an extreme, the threat of war would do more to integrate budgets, defence forces, and the capital goods and transport sectors, than a thousand proposals from the Commission ever could. In the absence of such an unexpected and undesirable kick-start, however, the progression from monetary union to commonplace sweeping fiscal transfers across national boundaries appears, shall we say, distinctly less than inexorable.

Back, now, to our unhappy electorates, which confronted with slowing growth, rising unemployment, and renewed calls for fiscal discipline, might well begin to blame both incumbent governments and the European Central Bank in equal measure. The former would naturally look for a scapegoat, and find it in the latter; and national politicians' increasingly vocal criticism of both 'Frankfurt' and 'Brussels' would only fan latent anti-EMU sentiment.

Eventually, in this scenario, the cost of remaining in EMU, measured in political self-interest and opinion poll rankings, becomes too large to bear. National control of monetary policy is dragged back from the ECB, and national banknotes are repossessed (if pre-2002) or reprinted (if post-2002). While EMU per se does not necessarily fall apart immediately, its contraction to little more than a core DM-zone does little to aid smooth relations between France and Germany, not least because the depreciation of the departing countries' new currencies prompts French demands for intra-EU protectionism. Ultimately, France too departs; and an always politically-driven project expires, with a neat twist of symmetry, on fundamentally politically motivated grounds.

Being pushed out of EMU

Most unsustainable EMU scenarios also allow for jumping governments to be given a helping hand by the financial markets (the 'speculators'). The risk of this is generally perceived to be highest during the initial three and a half years of EMU's life, during which toddling phase national banknotes will still exist, albeit only as fixed denominations of the same currency. The ability to pull out of EMU is, nevertheless, regarded as greater while national notes are still around to go back to. Investors, being aware of this, will therefore prefer to guard against even the slightest danger of a 'jump' by holding, for example, euro-DM instead of euro-lira on the grounds that, were EMU to fold, the German currency would be the safer bolt-hole. This inexorable shift into euro-DM notes irritates an innately Eurosceptic Bundesbank, and each display of irritation only encourages further flows of funds in its direction. The system eventually gives way even before the introduction of the new notes and coins, when the German central bank's willingness to go along with what it has always regarded as an inherently inadvisable course of action finally snaps.

Back to reality

The latter of these scenarios has, in the actual context of the late 1990s, no merit whatsoever. The jumping hypothesis does, however, bear careful attention, though not for the conclusions which its protagonists generally draw. First, however, to push the 'push' out of the picture.

Speculative attacks can certainly break fixed exchange rates, as Europe, Asia and Latin America can all testify. As the Bank of England's Willem Buiter has so succinctly put it: a fixed but adjustable peg is an accident waiting to happen. And happen, it almost always does. A single currency is not, however, simply an advanced version of a fixed exchange rate. EMU is not the ERM grown up, though the inability to grasp this has regrettably stymied much Eurosceptical thinking, especially on the northern side of the Channel.

If the entire world prefers to hold euro-DM notes rather than euro-lira, then that is what the entire world will hold; monetary policy makers will lose no sleep over the matter. The EMU money supply will not change, and if consumers and investors prefer to hold one particular design of banknote, this will be of no more relevance to central bankers than if Canadian investors suddenly took a liking to C$ banknotes printed in Toronto rather than in Quebec. There is no link to break between Toronto and Quebec banknotes, because there is no market. It is the same currency, watched over by the same central bank; and this will be equally true of EMU.

Investors may — will — speculate on Italian bonds versus German bonds, or Italian stocks versus French ones. Trading euros against the US dollar or sterling will also keep the wolf from many an investor's door, but there will be no speculation between the EMU currencies themselves, for the simple reason that there will be no intra-EMU markets to speculate in. A fixed link between sterling and the DM can be broken; but how to break the link between the Toronto C$ and the Quebec C$? The concept is meaningless; the market does not exist to be broken. Governments can resign from EMU, but the currency markets cannot push them — unless, of course, the central banks provide a shove of their own.

That the Bundesbank might itself help create an intra-EMU currency market by appearing to hesitate in its obligations would be laughable if it were not occasionally taken seriously. Whatever the previous misgivings of individual central bankers, the Bundesbank will carry out to the letter what its government has signed up to (on occasions, perhaps, a little more rigorously than that government might prefer). Furthermore, the Bundesbank will be a part of an ECB which it itself helped to design; theories of it having a private agenda betray both an over-fertile imagination and a shocking lack of familiarity with the personalities involved. If EMU breaks, it will not be because the central bankers have failed to stick to their script.

A final consideration from the speculators' angle is that, even if EMU were to fall apart for entirely unrelated reasons, it is by no means clear that overseas hoarders of euro-DM would be any better off than their euro-lira holding counterparts. There would not necessarily be any obligation on the Bundesbank to recognise speculative euro-DM held outside Germany as equivalent to the new post-EMU German currency. Legally, there would be no connection. Speculators would be holding old euro-notes, not the resurrected domestic German currency. The latter would not be capable of resurrection, however much the pictures on the banknotes might suggest otherwise. From January 1999, there is no going back to the systems and entities of 1998. Furthermore, a newly empowered Bundesbank might not feel too kindly disposed towards those who had hoped to profit from the collapse of a project which it had spent so many years helping to create.

If member states cannot be forced out of EMU by currency speculation in the same way that they could be forced out of the ERM, this does not of course mean that they cannot jump. (And currency speculation could, certainly, be a contributory factor here, in the sense that were the markets to push the euro down sharply against the US dollar, an ECB response incorporating higher interest rates would do few favours for already beleaguered EMU governments.) The flaws in the jumping argument do not lie in the description of the pressures facing members states in the event of a cyclical slowdown. The chain of events referred too above is, unfortunately, all too plausible; and the question of how to tackle an EMU backlash when growth next stalls should rank high on the list of priorities of any EMU government able to stretch its horizons beyond its next year's budget.

Where the jumping argument falters is in its underestimation of the difficulties of making the leap. Withdrawing from EMU would not be impossible. Although there is no allowance for it in the Maastricht Treaty, a country could scarcely be kept in against its will. Pulling out would, however, be an entirely different ball-game from withdrawal from the ERM. In practice it is difficult to envisage the circumstances under which any government would see such a leap in the dark as being preferable to staying put.

Once EMU starts, the effect on its participants is akin to that of an accelerating car on its passengers. However bumpy the journey gets, the risks of jumping out become greater with each passing moment. Far wiser to tighten the seatbelt and hold on, however scary the driving may become. The pros and cons of staying out of EMU are thus totally different from those of leaving EMU. Once a country joins, the balance tilts massively in favour of the status quo. In the face of such asymmetry, strains on individual countries, or outside shocks, such as the Asian crisis, are if anything likely to encourage greater, not less, integration.

It is reasonable to assume that a member state withdrawing from EMU would be unlikely to do so because its economy was performing too well. Furthermore, and whatever its actual preference on the matter, its exit would be perceived by outsiders as reflecting the wish to have a lower exchange rate and/or lower interest rates and/or a more expansive fiscal policy.

This is not a combination which usually impresses bond markets. Higher long term interest rates would be the instant penalty of EMU exit, with the new domestic rate incorporating a higher risk premium. The government would be seen as no longer subject to the monetary and fiscal disciplines imposed on EMU members: currency risk would have resurfaced; the markets would be nervous that one major about-turn in policy might simply be the first of many; and the government itself would probably not be looking particularly strong or stable. And if rising long term interest rates on its government debt were not enough, the withdrawing administration might also have to contend with rising short term interest rates. An independent central bank, with its monetary sovereignty newly restored, would almost certainly wish to take a cautious and credibility-enhancing stance in the face of a soft currency, an unpredictable fiscal outlook, and nervous financial markets. And if the government were to take the interest rate prerogative away from the ECB — only to keep it to itself, rather than handing it on to a domestic central bank — the stratospheric level of long term bond yields would quickly squeeze the economy far more effectively than even the most extreme independent central banker would ever have contemplated.

It is not just the market consequences of EMU exit which would give pause for thought; the practicalities, too, would be nightmarish. Once again, it must be stressed that they would not render withdrawal impossible, but they certainly put it into the category of the extremely improbable.

Pulling out of EMU would, as noted earlier, require the creation of an entirely new currency. Even if euro-DM or euro-lira banknotes still existed, the old currency would be legally and clinically dead. Bonds, bank accounts, mortgages, loans, indeed any national asset previously denominated in euro, would overnight be denominated in the new currency. For purely domestic assets, such as house mortgages, this would not be a major problem; but when it came to government debt held by overseas investors, the sudden switch of the base currency could keep the legal profession in profit for many a year. Conventional financial practice has always been to recognise the 'state theory of money' — that is, that the sovereign power which issues the money has jurisdiction over what constitutes that money. The French, German or British currency is, accordingly, whatever the French, German or British government says it is, a convention central to the smooth introduction of EMU itself, in that the substitution of euros for francs, marks or pounds is not regarded as altering existing contracts.

In the event of an amicable and mutually agreed EMU exit, the decision as to whether, for example, euro bonds should be repaid in euros or in the new domestic currency would be complicated but probably do-able. Sovereignty over national money would clearly have been given back to the national government concerned. Non-negotiated withdrawal, a unilateral termination of the Maastricht obligations by one member state, would, however, be a much greyer and murkier area. Some countries, whether EMU members or not, might refuse, albeit probably only temporarily, to recognise the new currency; and in the far more volatile environment of a non-negotiated and chaotic withdrawal, all lenders, sympathetic or not, would have every interest in insisting on being repaid only in euros.

Add to this the time-consuming process of trying to withdraw capital and reserves from the ECB; the risk of capital flight, and of a credit crunch not remediable by lower interest rates, even if the latter were forthcoming, which would be unlikely; the threat of protectionism from EMU members now faced with a soft currency competitor (and to echo our opening remark: while protectionism is not supposed to happen within the EU, too many impossible things have happened over the past decade to remain entirely sanguine in this regard); the probability that the accompanying chaos would have pushed up euro interest rates as a whole, dampening economic growth further; and the lack of certainty that the national electorate would show any gratitude whatsoever at the next elections towards a government whose EMU policy had so dramatically failed. Confronted with all of the above, even the most pressured government might prefer to devote the effort required to jump to pushing instead for a more expansionary fiscal or monetary stance from the inside.

But will it work?

That something survives does not mean that it succeeds. However great the economic and political strains, EMU itself is likely to be the very last link in the chain to give way. This is not necessarily a comfortable thought. It is, after all, entirely possible that the necessary structural reforms to cope with the newly competitive environment might not be quickly forthcoming, or that EMU policy makers in the ECB and in the Council of the euro Eleven proved unable to communicate and cooperate, resulting in a consistently inappropriate fiscal/monetary policy mix. Under such circumstances, Europe might be better off if EMU were a little less sustainable.

Fortunately, the risk of the ECB pursuing an initially over-aggressive course in the interests of credibility has been much reduced by the actual circumstances of late 1998. EMU has, to some extent, created the favourable conditions for its own birth. Short term interest rates are being pulled down across the EMU zone to a level suitable to the needs of the 52% of the EMU economy represented by France and Germany.

The fiscal squeeze of 1997 has, meanwhile, been reduced by the happy accident that recovering growth makes criteria carelessly expressed as headline deficit ratios, much easier to meet. If asset prices and domestic demand are booming in areas such as Ireland, this is a problem for Ireland; not for the ECB. Local difficulties in a corner of the EMU bloc accounting for 1% of the EMU economy, are not going to shape ECB policy. Mix in to all of the above, the dampening effects on headline inflation and growth of the Asian slowdown, and the ECB starts life with far less to do on the interest rate front than appeared likely even a year previously.

That the ECB's arrival is proving rather smoother than had been feared does not, however, guarantee its longer term success, though success is a rather woolly concept to define. The Maastricht Treaty did its best. EMU's success would be recognised by balanced, non-inflationary, and environmentally-friendly economic growth; by a high level of employment and social well-being; by steadily improving living standards; by broader competition; and by general economic and social cohesion across the EMU bloc. The drafters of the Treaty certainly cannot be faulted for a lack of ambition. It is, however, perhaps fairer to judge EMU's success in relative rather than absolute terms, comparing it with the realistic available alternatives; an exercise which will clearly have a large subjective component, and never therefore be truly convincing.

If postwar Europe had been a fully employed, low-inflation collection of nation states and floating currencies, EMU would never have made it off the drawing board. No-one can pretend that EMU was inspired simply by the search for lower transaction costs and a wish to drive foreign exchange bureaux out of business; it has always had a blueprint that goes beyond the economic. Of course, EMU was a political project — which does not thereby make it right or wrong; and of course, on the economic front, it has become a means of introducing competition and forcing through the structural changes which were supposed to precede union, but which national governments themselves have been too weak to implement. If Euroland fails to reach the heights described in the Treaty and summarised in the previous paragraph, this does not however mean that the project has failed. It may still have been better than the alternatives.

Success, in its relative sense, will always be in the eye of the beholder. For some, EMU will never be successful; their perceived hypothetical alternative would always have outperformed in any environment. Equally, a minority will always be convinced that things would invariably have been worse without EMU. For most politicians and voters, however, their judgement on EMU's success will fluctuate with their own feel-good factor; and for a new institution such as the ECB, forced to build up its popular legitimacy from a standing start, being seen to succeed by this majority will be just as important as succeeding. Transparency and accountability matter; but as the Bundesbank has shown (and do not forget that the Bundesbank itself began life not as a product of German consensus, but of a trial of strength between the UK and US, and that the DM was the ultimate political currency), nothing succeeds like success.

We have already referred to the risk of a popular backlash against both the ECB and incumbent governments once economic growth slows and unemployment ratchets up. The better the success rating which the ECB has earned in the interim, the more difficult it will be for weak national governments to use Frankfurt as a scapegoat. A foreign-based institution is, unfortunately, always going to be an easy target for national politicians in a tight spot, as the European Parliament and the Commission can attest. The strains which slowing growth will place on mainstream political parties should not be underestimated; the temptation to deflect some of the electorate's discontent overseas, will be immense.

Virtually the whole continental European political mainstream has been pro-EMU. The entire political centre, and not just governments, will therefore attract some of the blame when the economic cycle next tips down, leaving as beneficiaries primarily the parties of the extreme right and left. As local and regional elections in France, Germany and elsewhere in the late 1990s have shown, these parties are already quite capable of making life very uncomfortable for their mainstream counterparts, even where electoral systems preclude their gaining much direct power at a national level.

Sustainable EMU

EMU is sustainable. While its longevity cannot be predicted as confidently as death and taxes, the extremely high costs of exit, and the tendency of external shocks to only encourage further integration, both argue in its favour.

There is, however, nothing inherently good in sustainability per se. In the event of a consistently inappropriate policy mix, one might wish that EMU had rather less staying power; and even the most optimistic scenario has to allow for the fact that the structural changes which EMU will, and is intended to impose may be transition costs for the economy, but will feel all too permanent to the individuals affected.

When European growth slows, voter sentiment will turn; the only question, is how sharply and within how large a section of the electorate. The risk, then, is not of national governments jumping out of EMU, or even of the markets expecting any to do so, but of weak political parties, under attack from the extremes of right and left, trying to deflect some of the blame for rising unemployment onto 'Europe' and the Central Bank. By damaging such legitimacy as that institution may by then have gained, and by doing little to encourage the flow of information and cooperation between the ECB and the euro Eleven finance ministers, which will be central to effective EMU policy-making, such buck-passing would only exacerbate an already difficult economic situation — without necessarily saving the political skins of the individuals concerned.

Will EMU survive? Almost certainly. Will it succeed? Probably; though the applause may come rather hollow from those individuals and regions which will bear the bulk of the adjustment costs. And will a successful EMU be recognised and appreciated as such by European voters in two, five, or ten years time? Perhaps; though only if national politicians have, in the interim, been uncharacteristically generous, giving the ECB ample credit for any economic success, while refraining from laying the entire blame for economic disappointment at Frankfurt's door. EMU will almost certainly survive and will probably succeed; but when it comes to being seen to have succeeded, even a committed pro-European must be forgiven a twinge of scepticism.

---

[1] Mitchell Madison Group, WSJE 15 July 1998; fund managers controlling £1.1tr, or 40% of assets under management in the UK.

3. Affording EMU

Iain Begg

The contention is that economic and monetary union will cost a fortune, and someone will have to pay the bill. Once the EU currencies are irrevocably locked together, there are bound to be new demands for public spending to deal with the consequences of monetary union. Higher unemployment compensated by over-generous benefits, unfunded pensions, production of new notes and coins, asymmetric shocks and conversion of machines are just some of the costs that will be incurred because of EMU. The Greeks, the Spaniards and the Portuguese, not to mention the Italians, will want much more for regional policy. And if you believe what you read and hear, the British taxpayer will be stung for all of these costs.

The exchequer costs of EMU

Is any of this true? As with so much to do with EMU, there is a grain of truth mixed up with a confusion about how monetary union will function. On a strict interpretation of what has been agreed, taxation and public expenditure decisions (fiscal policy) will remain the responsibility of member states when monetary policy moves 'upwards' to be administered by the European Central Bank. This means that although the Stability and Growth Pact will oblige governments to curb their budget deficits, 'Brussels' will not be able to dictate how public money is spent. The exception to this is the budget of the European Union itself over which the EU institutions notionally have control, although it is important to recognise that the EU budget is pretty inflexible with most of its spending going on agricultural policy and regional assistance.

In principle, there is no reason for the single currency to increase the cost of belonging to the EU club. There are no proposals to increase the EU budget beyond its current ceiling of 1.27% of GDP. In its 1997 communication *Agenda 2000*, the European Commission put forward plans for the EU's medium-term financial framework beyond the current mandate which expires in 1999. These plans will, broadly, maintain the status quo.[1] Indeed, the early skirmishes suggest that several member states are keen to cut the budget.

It follows that there is no obvious, immediate reason for EMU to give rise to a burden on the British Exchequer, irrespective of whether or not the UK joins the single currency. Rather, the fears about the cost of EMU centre on expectations that those dastardly Europeans will move on to the next project and that this will lead inexorably to a larger central budget.

This chapter considers why and how EMU might give rise to demands on national exchequers. In doing so, it attempts to distinguish the probable and possibly desirable from the fanciful and the downright dishonest. The starting point is that in any economic space there are good reasons for the highest level of government to have some budgetary autonomy, just as it sometimes makes sense to devolve power. That frequently traduced concept, subsidiarity, cuts both ways.

Fiscal federalism

Economists have devoted considerable effort to working out optimal arrangements between tiers of government for tax-raising and public expenditure.[2] These theories of fiscal federalism usually assume a powerful central government, whether in a unitary state or a federal system, with the highest level of government exercising significant control over macroeconomic policy and, often, the distribution of national income and wealth. The financing of lower levels of government then falls between two options:

• where the central government controls all the taxes and makes grants to sub-national tiers of governments to cover their outlays;

• where sub-national government owns taxes sufficient to cover all its expenditure.

What makes the EU unusual is that the highest level of government, the supranational level, has little say over the fiscal arrangements of lower tiers. Moreover, it is largely dependent on them for its financial resources. This is not a system that has any real parallels, although the German Reich from 1871 to 1918 has been cited as an example of a third model in which the central government receives the bulk of its revenue from lower tiers.[3] The EU level of government plainly falls well short of the federal tiers found, for example, in the USA or Germany, but is instead somewhere between an international organisation (such as the United Nations) and the highest level of government. This is, arguably, unique and means that formal economic models do not lend themselves readily to the analysis of EU budgetary arrangements.

Political scientists, too, disagree on the nature of the EU, with some arguing that it is still, essentially, an intergovernmental organisation while others consider it an altogether more ambitious complement to other levels of governance.

These are not, however, purely academic debates. Wyplosz observes that 'currencies and nations normally coincide'.[4] It can be argued that the advent of the single currency will not only break new ground in economic management, but will also challenge the current distribution of budgetary powers.

Adjustment to economic shocks

One of the key challenges facing the EU is how to make EMU function effectively. We can guess that the ECB will pursue policies similar to those that the Bundesbank has traditionally followed and that governments will be unwilling or unable to countenance large budget deficits. The outlook for stability objectives such as containing inflation should, consequently, be favourable. Advocates of monetary orthodoxy would argue, further, that this in itself will be sufficient to assure a greatly economic improved performance. But it does not necessarily allow for automatic or easy correction of economic problems in parts of the EU. This raises the question of how the EMU policy framework needs to be reshaped to permit effective adjustment of economies.

The glib answer is labour market flexibility, with the US often cited as the model Europe should try to emulate. But 'third way' or not, the idea that it is virtuous labour market flexibility that enables the US to achieve internal adjustment is far-fetched. What is overlooked is the critical role played by fiscal transfers. In any advanced economy, the interplay between the tax system and public expenditure dampens fluctuations in economic activity. In most economies, the stabilising transfers are automatic: when a regional economy is in the doldrums, tax revenue falls off so that less is paid to central government, but receipts from social security programmes funded by central government tend to increase. Estimates for the US suggest that more than half of the potential downturn in regional income is averted in this way.[5]

The problem for the European Union is that tax and benefit systems are not integrated so that these automatic stabilisers do not function as they do in most countries. Nor is labour market flexibility either sufficient to compensate, or likely to become so. There are three ways of interpreting this, all of which have surfaced in the EMU debate:

• The first is the argument that, because EMU lacks such mechanisms, it will be so vulnerable to shocks that its credibility and sustainability will be undermined. If the benefits of EMU fail (as they inevitably will fail) to reach parts of the economy that policies such as devaluation reach, some regions will face prolonged disequilibrium, unless other policy measures are adopted. In extremis, this would result in EMU imploding.

• Second, it is argued that stabilisation mechanisms within countries are sufficiently powerful to deal with regional shocks affecting part of them, and that this will not materially be altered by monetary union.[6] The obvious flaw in this is that the adversely affected 'region' could be an entire member state. Finland, for example, went through a very difficult period at the beginning of the 1990s. Certainly, there are powerful stabilisation mechanisms in the larger EU member states that do help to moderate regional shocks, but it would be foolhardy to claim that these will suffice to cope with severe disequilibrium such as that engendered by the cyclical disjunction between the UK and German economies in the early 1990s.

• The third option is to argue that EMU needs to arm itself with automatic stabilisers if it is to be viable in the long-term. And it is here that the fears about not being able to afford EMU become real. If the EU is to be endowed with the capacity to respond, it will need financial resources substantially greater than it has at present. This was mooted as long ago as 1977 in the MacDougall report and a number of schemes for its implementation have been explored.[7]

If the third option is favoured, a great deal of thought will need to go into the design of sensible policy machinery. This is not the place for a detailed discussion of how this can be achieved, but it will almost certainly involve reform of the EU budget.

The EU budget

Mathematicians are accustomed to numbers with mystical properties. Even those with the most hazy memories of geometry are familiar with p which, combined with r^2 gives the area of a circle. The constant e is central to an understanding of calculus. Now, it seems, the figure 1.27 has become the magical figure for the EU budget. Since 1993 it has been the agreed ceiling for the budget as a percentage of GDP, and the proposals published in *Agenda 2000* envisage it remaining until 2006. Even this amount, modest by the standards of public expenditure in most countries, is now being challenged by several member states concerned to curb their net contribution to the EU. This is despite the fact that the Treaty states that the Union shall be financed by the proceeds of 'own resources', that is, taxes that 'belong' to the EU.

What is not seriously discussed is what the EU budget ought to do, and how big or small it should be to fulfil its role. The budget has evolved as much as the result of compromises and deals as any grand design. Brigid Laffan puts it this way:

'The public finances of the Union lie at the borderline between politics and economics, between market integration and political union, wider economic integration and political union'.[8]

In the aftermath of the fiscal squeezes that most member states have been through in order to meet the EMU convergence criteria, budgetary rigour is in order. But while the politics of paying less are readily understandable, the economics of the EU budget are much more dubious.

The European Union aspires to be an integrated economy with common policies. Even if the term subsidiarity had never been coined, some of these policies should be carried out at the member state level or by sub-national tiers of government. Others are conducted more effectively at supranational level; indeed, the logic of monetary union is that it will be easier to achieve the goals of monetary policy by having a common currency. The debate on the merits of monetary union has gone on ad nauseam and is not worth revisiting, but what has been conspicuously absent is a rational discussion of whether the move to EMU should be accompanied by changes in budgetary policy.

So far, the answer has been coordination of member states' policies either through Ecofin, the Council of the finance ministers of the member states, or the Euro Council, the informal body comprising just the first wave members of EMU. The trouble with this arrangement is that it leaves decisions on how EMU is conducted vulnerable to disputes between member states on the fiscal policies that suit them. There is no guarantee that the combination of national fiscal policies will complement the stance of monetary policy, nor that the mix of monetary and fiscal policy will be what the EU economy requires.

The obvious alternative is to increase the scale and scope of the central EU budget to make it viable as a fiscal counterweight to the ECB. Howls of protest would, no doubt, greet any such proposal, so that it is important to be clear on the economic functions that the EU budget might reasonably be expected to fulfil. If the aim is macroeconomic stabilisation, the EU would need to be able to raise or lower its spending to influence aggregate demand. The corollary is that it would require authority to borrow, even if it were obliged to balance the books over that slippery notion, the economic cycle. Estimates from DG II of the Commission suggest that, together with the stabilisation policies of national governments, much could be achieved with a fund of the order of 0.3% of EU GDP.[9]

A second main justification for a larger EU budget is the likely demands on the supranational level to respond to inequalities between regions, especially if these are perceived to have been aggravated by EMU. The Commission is already called upon to advance economic and social cohesion through the structural funds and will acquire new obligations as the EU expands eastwards. These policies fall under the heading of structural operations because their purpose is to enhance the long-term development of the economy. This has to be distinguished from a third rationale that is commonly used to justify expenditure by the highest tier of government, namely redistribution. If the propositions of fiscal federalism are accepted, a persuasive case could be made for cross-border payments to boost the incomes of less-favoured areas, but in the EU at present, transfers for this purpose must be regarded as implausible.

Although *Agenda 2000* cleverly paves the way for enlargement without increasing the budget as a percentage of GDP, the proposals make no allowance for any EMU-related demands on the budget. It is, therefore, likely to be severely stretched unless the weight of agricultural spending is reduced. It is important in exploring the case for a larger budget to assess what the EU level is best suited to do. This, in turn, calls for a careful look at the areas of public spending and taxation that could reasonably be 'Europeanised'.

On the expenditure side, there are various network projects (for example in transport, telecommunications and energy), some of which are already funded under the TENs initiative, which could be brought forward. These, however, are long-term in character and would not be suitable for stabilisation purposes, although they support economic development and the overall competitiveness of the EU. For stabilisation purposes, outlays linked to the economic cycle are needed and an idea that has surfaced a number of times is to create a fund linked to unemployment.[10] This would have to be carefully designed to reflect national differences in labour market institutions and thus to be fair to all sides, but from a macroeconomic standpoint, the key requirement would be that the fund should act in a contra-cyclical manner.

Dealing comprehensively with so-called asymmetric shocks would require more substantial transfers than are likely to be politically acceptable in today's EU, unlike in Germany where, despite some grumbling, transfers to the former DDR were. The Union could, nevertheless, contribute to alleviating the impact of shocks by having discretion to accelerate expenditure in areas where there is a 'European' policy interest. For example, there could be budget lines for environmental projects or for inter-regional cooperation to promote social cohesion. The fundamental point, though, is not to be unduly prescriptive in specifying new public expenditure, but to recognise that EU level expenditure, together with the taxation raised to finance it, has a role to play in the EMU policy framework.

Genuine own resources for the EU?

On the revenue side, it is not just the scale of payments but how they are levied that matters. Moreover, a critical obstacle to clear-headed thinking on the EU budget is that member states continue to regard it as their own money. Mrs Thatcher's long guerrilla war over the budget was only the most visible sign of a pervasive cult in the EU of *juste retour* – the insistence on seeing a financial return for what is put in. This means that the member states can hold the EU institutions to ransom by making noises about reducing contributions, notwithstanding the Treaty commitment to endow the union with its own resources. At present, just 17% of the EU revenue comes from trade duties, the so-called traditional own resources. The biggest tranche of EU revenue comes from a share of the proceeds of VAT in member states, with the balance made up from a GNP related transfer.

This has long troubled the European Parliament which has campaigned for a more transparent and visible system of financing the Union.[11] But here again the proposals in *Agenda 2000* are for a retention of the status quo. Although there would be winners and losers from any change, the problem is not one of finding a suitable tax base: plenty of options have been canvassed over the years. Rather, it is one of control, with member states unwilling to cede any fiscal powers, so that previous attempts to introduce new revenue instruments for the EU have been thwarted. There is, nevertheless, good reason for giving the EU authentic own resources. This would result in greater certainty on income and make it easier for the EU level to determine priorities for the Union as a whole, rather than being subject to pressures, tacit or explicit, to provide a *juste retour* to member states.

Any new own resource has to have a number of attributes if it is to stand a chance of being acceptable to the member states. Key ones are being a buoyant and sufficient source of revenue, equitable between member states, and economically efficient. Political *desiderata* include visibility to tax-payers, a link with European policies and avoiding upsetting member state sensitivities as might happen if direct taxes on personal incomes were under consideration. Among the many options for new own resources that have been canvassed, two that have the potential to be developed as long term solutions are a 'carbon tax' and a common corporation tax.

The original conception of the carbon tax idea was a levy on production of energy using fossil fuels. Its greatest merit is that it would be a direct response to a common concern. It would, however, fall most heavily on heavy manufacturing regions, and if it succeeded in its environmental aims, the proceeds of the tax could fall. What is more, because France generates a significantly higher than average proportion of its energy from nuclear power, the French would pay less. A variant on the scheme that seems to this author to make more sense would be to tax energy consumption, most straightforwardly by an excise on vehicle fuel.

As the single market becomes increasingly integrated (and even the most diehard of euro-sceptics tends to concede that the single market is a worthwhile objective), identification of where corporate profits arise will become harder. If corporate tax regimes differ, the tax can distort competition. A common corporation tax can, therefore, be justified as a measure consistent with the single market as well as being a viable source of revenue. Its drawbacks are, essentially, practical rather than issues of principle. At present member states tax profits in varying ways and are reluctant to harmonise these procedures. There are, nevertheless, moves afoot to bring these tax regimes closer together, so that in the years to come the obstacles to corporate taxation as an own resource should diminish.[12]

In the meantime, VAT could be revamped to make it more visible as a European tax by the simple expedient of distinguishing the EU component from the domestic one. And, being a little imaginative, there are levies that could, relatively painlessly, be reassigned to the EU as own resources. Airport taxes, for instance, are now charged in all countries, albeit at differing rates. Given that much of the traffic is intra-European and that air transport has become a European policy matter, a good case could be made for making this an own resource. Perfectly viable own resources can, in short, be found; what is missing is the political will to introduce them.

Coins, machines, software and pensions

That there will be costs in making the transition to EMU is undeniable, raising yet another dimension of affording EMU. Some one-off costs, such as conversion of coin-operated machines, printing of new notes and coins, and adaptation of commercial software are unavoidable. In practice what will happen is that replacements or upgradings will occur sooner than they would otherwise, so that there is a real cost, though not a disproportionate one. Although some financial intermediaries, in particular, have voiced concern about the cost of all this at much the same time as they have to deal with the millennium computer bug, it would be disingenuous to claim that this made EMU unaffordable.

If some of the other claims about the costs of EMU were accurate, the verdict would be different. Social protection consumes an average of some 28% of GDP in the EU, so that if EMU implied sharing the responsibility for financing this, arguments about affordability would have great weight. However, the notion that British taxpayers will end up subsidising German pensions arises from yet another misconception about how EMU will function.

Germany (and other member states) has a social protection system in which the bulk of pensions are organised through the state, but with both sides of industry actively involved in their administration. Britain, by contrast, has much more developed occupational pensions which fund pensions directly. Pensions will, indeed, be a major headache for governments in the years to come. As the Federal Trust has shown, the pressures emanating from the ageing of society will make financing these systems increasingly problematic.[13] Governments will be forced to choose between curbing entitlements or finding new ways of raising the required revenue. In an international context in which labour costs (especially the non-wage element accounted for largely by the social security contributions that fund pensions) are coming under pressure, for reasons of competitiveness, there are few options open to governments.

51

The misconception here is that if certain EMU members have difficulty in meeting their budgetary targets, they will be able to borrow cheaply from the ECB and thereby support their pensioners at other people's expense. What this overlooks is the no bail-out rule which means that such borrowing is simply not permitted. If governments cannot reform their pension systems they will either have to cut other public spending or raise taxes. Either way, it is not the British taxpayer who will come to the rescue.

Can we afford it?

Increasing the size of the EU budget, even if it can be shown that it would allow EMU to function more effectively, cannot but be contentious. Affordability is not, however, the primary question. If governments choose to assign more powers to Brussels, they would have to give the institutions the means to carry them out – and that means a bigger budget requiring higher contributions. But provided the enlarged budget facilitated more effective economic management, it would be money well spent. Transferring functions from one level of government to another would only cost more if there were good reason to expect the reassignment to lead to less efficient administration. Moreover, despite its reputation in the UK, the European Commission is a reasonably high calibre and well-run bureaucracy. It has its faults and we certainly hear about them, but it is important not to allow either a (possibly understandable) desire to cling to national institutions, however outdated, or simple misinformation to colour judgements about reform.

In conclusion, there is no compelling reason for EMU to result in higher public expenditure in the EU, or indeed, for individual member states to have to pay more. In that sense, there is no issue about whether we can afford EMU. Some restructuring of public spending ought, nevertheless, to be contemplated, and good reasons can be put forward for reassigning more public functions to the European level. This would mean bigger transfers to Europe, but would be offset by lower domestic spending, so that affording EMU would largely be a matter of robbing Peter to pay Paul.

Monetary union is undoubtedly a big step to take and one that will only deliver the anticipated benefits if the policy framework as a whole is sensibly constructed. Perhaps the dilemma of EMU is not whether we can afford it but whether we can afford not to fund it adequately.

[1] European Commission, *Agenda 2000: For a stronger and wider Union*, Bulletin of the European Union, Supplement 5/97.

[2] See, for example, W.E. Oates, *Studies in Fiscal Federalism*, London, Edward Elgar, 1991; and European Commission, 'The economics of Community public finance', *European Economy* reports and studies, No. 5, 1993.

[3] B. Eichengreen and J. von Hagen, 'Fiscal policy and monetary union: federalism, fiscal restrictions and the no-bail-out rule', CEPR Discussion Paper No. 1247, 1995.

[4] Charles Wyplosz, 'EMU: why and how it might happen' in *Journal of Economic Perspectives*, 11, 3-22, 1997.

[5] Tamim Bayoumi and Paul R. Masson, 'Fiscal Flows in the United States and Canada: Lessons for Monetary Union in Europe' in *European Economic Review*, 39(2), February 1995, pp. 253-74.

[6] For example, European Commission, 1993, op. cit.

[7] See Iain Begg and François Nectoux 'The social consequences of EMU' in *Journal of European Social Policy*, 1995; and for a discussion of the possible role of the EU budget, P. Bernd Spahn, *The Community Budget for an Economic and Monetary Union,* Basingstoke, Macmillan 1993.

[8] Brigid Laffan, *The Finances of the European Union*, Basingstoke, Macmillan, 1997, p. 15.

[9] Alexander Italianer and Marc Vanheukelen, 'Proposals for Community stabilisation mechanisms: some historical applications' in *The Economics of Community Public Finance, European Economy* special issue, 1992.

[10] Some of these are discussed in Begg and Nectoux, op. cit.

[11] I. Begg, N. Grimwade and P. Price with E. Lally, *The Own Resources of the European Union: Analysis and Possible developments*, Luxembourg, European Parliament, Directorate-General for Research, Working Document, Budget Series W-4, 1997.

[12] In the 1997 Action Plan for the Single Market.

[13] Dick Taverne, Federal Trust Report, *The Pension Time Bomb in Europe*, London, Federal Trust, 1995.

4. Investing in Euroland

Graham Bishop [1]

This analysis is split into two parts: the scale and development of the financial markets of the 'ins', and the significance of being outside Euroland.

THE SCALE OF EUROLAND

The euro Eleven has a bigger population than that of the USA, and the GDP of the Eleven is a little smaller than the US currently. But if Euroland eventually covers the whole of the EU, it will have a bigger economy than the US. If Eastern and Central Europe come in, its population will be roughly twice that of the US.

For portfolio investors in the financial markets rather than direct investment, the government bond markets are key. In the table overleaf, the term 'bonds' has a very specific definition in our index, that is, fixed rate with more than one year remaining life, thus excluding much Italian debt. Many international investors use the Salomon Smith Barney World Government Bond Index as their benchmark. In just about sixty business days, the European governments' bond market will be roughly the same size as the US Treasury market. If the UK joins, with Denmark, Sweden and Greece, then the European market would be significantly bigger.

So Euroland is a big event for the world's financial system, because a new, global market is coming into existence. The preparations are intense. The Bank of England, perhaps surprisingly for an 'out' central bank, has been pursuing a very active policy of ensuring that the City of London, a cornerstone of the European financial system, is fully involved with the preparations. The sheer scale of preparations is unreported by the media, but the intention is to turn the European Union's capital market, in the remaining business days, into a simple, transparent, harmonised market that can look the US Treasury market in the eye as a straightforward competitor.

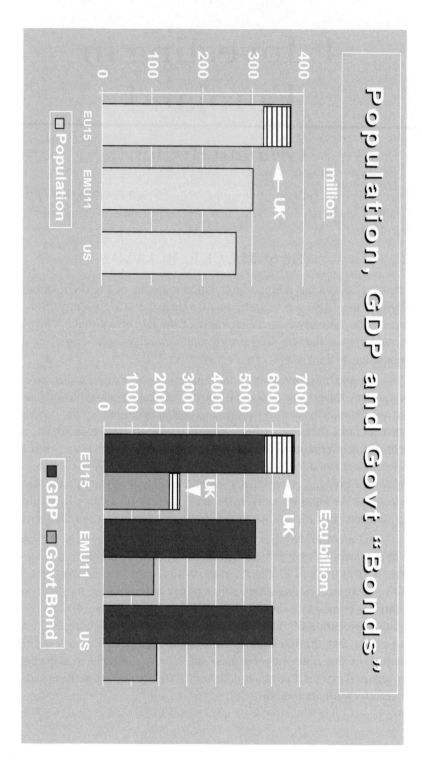

Population, GDP and Govt "Bonds"

Is the US Treasury bond market still such an absolute benchmark for the global investment flows associated with the world's reserve currency? Even in recent months, the Spanish government has built up its longer dated bond issue to about Ecu 14 bn. The current benchmark US Treasury ten-year is only Ecu 11 bn, and the size is now declining as the US budget is in surplus. The French government has, as a matter of policy over many years, built up the size of its fungible bonds (known as OATs) to about Ecu 15 bn; German government bonds in that maturity segment are also in the region of Ecu 15 bn. A number of government debt managers are increasing the size of their bonds with an implicit intention of making them as liquid (because they would be as large) as a US Treasury issue. In the early part of 1999, once the inevitable difficulties of this changeover are done, we will be looking at a euro-denominated government bond market which is as big, technically simple, and approaching the liquidity of the US Treasury market. That has tremendous implications for global markets which have not yet been fully taken on board.

The importance of securitisation

Analysing the possible development of the European financial system, a number of parallels can be drawn with the US, particularly its banking system. The share of credit extended by it, as a percentage of GDP, over the past twenty years has remained essentially unchanged. But the striking feature of the US financial system is the rise in total bonds as a percentage of GDP.

The most interesting aspect for Europe is that the growth of the US bond market has not been driven by the size of the government's deficit but by the non-Federal government sector. This enormous surge in non-government activity has included agencies, mortgage-backed bonds, corporate bonds, and Yankee (that is, foreign issuer) bonds — the latter reflecting the role of the dollar as a global reserve currency — as well as bonds backed by all sorts of financial assets, including credit cards, and even loans to small companies. In practice, virtually any financial asset which produces a predictable inflow of cash — a 'receivable' — can now be 'securitised'. This means that a bond can be issued, via the capital markets, that gives the lender the right to those cash flows.

The main factor in boosting the US bond market in the mid 1980s was the banking system's capital adequacy problems. In particular, banks like Citibank (now part of Citigroup) decided that the problems of capital inadequacy were so great that they needed to sell off some of the assets on their balance sheet. The chosen mechanism was to securitise it, thereby removing it from the balance sheet whilst retaining customer relationships by servicing the credit cards, etc.

The exposure of European banks to the emerging markets is surprising: an amount equal to 75% of their capital is so exposed. This has a historical resonance in the US where the same problem was also the driving force. To the extent that European banks experience any similar problems stemming from the emerging markets, there would be a force that could stimulate the growth of the securitised bond markets in Euroland. However, European banks collectively have enough problems at home to stimulate such developments, even without extra problems from the emerging markets. Starting from a similar base in the late 1970s, European bond markets have shown good growth, an increase of 80% in the value of bonds outstanding, but nowhere near the scale of the rocketing size of the US markets.

On 1 January 1999 the euro, at a stroke, abolishes currency matching rules which presently lock many countries' long-term savings institutions into domestic assets. For example, Europe's life insurance companies must match 80% of their assets to the currency of their liabilities. Until the end of 1998, the vast majority of those liabilities are denominated in national currency, as are most of the assets. Once those institutions can diversify their portfolios, they will be looking around Euroland for other investment opportunities that yield more than government bonds. Securitised assets should loom large on the menu of new opportunities, though it will take some years while that menu builds up. But there should be little doubt that that will happen eventually as companies disintermediate the banking system, avoiding the costs and relative inflexibility of bank loans, and go directly to the capital markets.

The implications of securitised credit in Euroland

Securitising European credit may create a profound, and perhaps quite rapid, change in the financial structure. Because of the differences between the short and long-term interest rate sensitivity of economies, the result could be a much more uniform financial structure right the way across Euroland. For example, judging by the speed with which UK citizens have shifted their mortgages to fixed rate — now up to 59% of new mortgages — fears about a different financial structure in the UK could dissipate within a surprisingly short number of years after British entry into EMU.

Who can issue? The traditional concept of a major company issuing a long term bond to a number of investors, such as life insurance companies, is already outmoded and will probably only be a fragment of the new market. There are likely to be two sources: pan-European banks and new types of issuer. Those banks with technologically sophisticated administrative and sales systems may be able to offer their products throughout Euroland, giving them a major competitive edge. This may prompt even more re-structuring of the European banking system. New types of issuer are already apparent from the US and UK models. Companies that wish to sell their products on credit are well placed to economise on working capital by selling the right to the customer's payments.

Regional government is another sector of potential issuers, though the relationship with central government will be a key factor in determining the cost of funds. A straightforward guarantee is one approach. Or the region may have the power to raise taxes separately from the central authority. Market participants will examine very carefully those constitutional arrangements to ensure that no adverse changes are likely during the life of any bond that may depend on those taxing powers for repayment. Alternatively, the regional government may wish to stimulate infrastructure projects that themselves generate cash-flows, the classic example being a toll road or bridge.

Many different models have been tried in the global markets and there seems little reason why these techniques cannot be imported into Euroland. The key is more likely to be whether investors develop a sufficient appetite for securities other than those issued by their own central government.

Who lends, and why? Long-term investors seek a reward commensurate with the risks they bear. For investors, the political commitment to budget discipline has been a vital step towards EMU because top quality government bonds, of the type that will exist in Euroland, are the foundation of many investment portfolios. However, financial markets of this scale cannot be controlled by an individual government but can act as a rolling referendum on the views of savers about the fiscal probity of a particular government. As the EU is founded on the principle of open and competitive markets, savers are free to move their funds to where they can get an adequate return for any risk perceived in answer to the simple question: will the state pay my interest and principal on time?

If there is any real doubt, a myriad of investment decisions taken by, or on behalf of, the ageing savers of Europe will roll those savings to safer havens. The European financial markets are no more than intermediaries for the retirement savings of ageing citizens, largely, of Europe. In a world of free movement of capital, any discipline over and above that of the electorate should come from the markets that finance any excess of spending, the national equivalent of the bank manager, rather than an external political power.

There can be no compulsion to lend because all EU members now have a liberal, market-based economic system. Moreover, the Treaty forbids it.[2] These institutions may seem anonymous and remote, but they are merely convenient legal channels in which to pool the retirement savings of the electorate. Pension funds, life insurance companies, unit trusts, and so on hold a large slice of a government's accumulated debts. Banks take deposits from the electorate and invest some of it in government debt as well.

The existence of very large and liquid capital markets may well have profound political implications for the EU. Investors will not feel themselves restricted to securities offered by their own government. Instead, they will have several competing governments and a profusion of non-government issuers, whether regional governments, traditional corporate bonds or new securitised issues that underpin innovative credit opportunities for the Euroland economy.

The euro as a global reserve currency. There are strong arguments for creating markets inside the EU that are as big as the US dollar markets. But will they be at all attractive to outsiders? Purchasing power parity calculations for the euro suggest that it will start life looking fairly cheap, in particular against the dollar. Current account surpluses are forecast to remain around 1% of GDP, and inflation is likely to equal that of the US, and the OECD area generally. This is good news for a firm euro. Investing in a currency with financial markets as developed as the dollar markets should provide an attractive set of opportunities. The euro, therefore, could quite rapidly develop the potential to become a reserve currency to challenge the dollar.

Another important force driving the creation of a reserve currency is whether or not the importers wish to continue to hold the currency once they have sold their goods. The European Union is a bigger trader with the rest of the world than the US. In the special case of Central and East European countries that want to come into the European Union, the obvious and natural policy for them is to hold euros. North Africa may well become part of the euro-zone; the Middle East, as a major supplier of oil, and Norway, selling gas into Europe, are all likely to find their trade denominated in euros over the next few years. So the question follows: what will those countries do with those euros they earn? They would be wise to hold them in the Euroland financial markets.

Future developments of the Euroland financial markets. One of the under-reported events at the informal Ecofin meeting at York in March 1998, was a request to the Commission to review the financial services legislation in order to make sure that the single market in finance is all that it should be. This was a call to modernise because the package of measures that created a single market in financial services, including the Second Banking Directive and the Investment Services Directive, were all designed ten years ago. Regrettably, the legislation is not yet in force in all countries because of delays in national implementation measures. Commissioner Monti has been active in spelling out these issues. Further progress was made at the European Council at Cardiff in June 1998. The summit's conclusions invited the Commission to table a framework for action by the time the Vienna European Council met in December. To quote the communiqué, these proposals should 'improve the single market in financial services, in particular examining the effectiveness of implementation of current legislation and identifying weaknesses which may require amending legislation'.

Part of the wide process of change reflects market developments; and it is surprising how little discussion there is in the media and the financial markets about the effect of technology on securities trading. At a basic level, securitisation is driven by technology: for example, the receivable of credit cards can easily be securitised. More interestingly, we are now in a position to use a PC anywhere around the world to log in, directly or via the internet, to Reuters, Bloomberg and various other services, and make a transaction on an equity market (and probably the bond market fairly soon). Such a transaction can be made on the market through an electronic auction, the security transferred and the payment made, all without any human intervention. The extraordinary speed, and associated reduction in costs, of this type of transaction is dramatic. The commercial implications may be as dramatic: the sudden death of LIFFE's contract on German government bonds illustrates the way in which trading patterns respond to the lower costs of electronic trading.

Lower costs should encourage more citizens to take the opportunity of being directly involved in equity markets. Perhaps most interesting to banks will be the significant number of savers who will be able to access government bond markets which have very large, liquid bonds. Will it be possible to do that through the internet, and will the governments themselves set up their own auction process so that any citizen can have direct access to those bonds?

There are some very interesting issues that now have to be addressed, which go to the heart of what is a financial market. What really is a stock exchange? It is only a set of electronic blips moving in conformity with a set of local regulations. But the electronic blips can go off to Frankfurt or to London, or to wherever it is easiest. Part of the purpose of the Commission review of financial services should be to ensure there are no legal impediments to the market developing the most efficient services possible to provide these services to the consumer in Euroland.

THE SIGNIFICANCE OF BEING OUT

For the 'in' commercial companies, the picture is very attractive: the euro will remove all currency risk and difficulties within Euroland and can be used outside as a reserve currency to ease exporting. Right the way across the relevant trading area, a company will have the same low interest rates and the same lack of interest rate volatility. However, there will be new risks in managing this economic area and they may pose difficulties. The task facing Britain's political leaders is to form a pragmatic and balanced view of the advantages and disadvantages of British participation.

Outside Euroland, in Britain, for example, a company will experience the mirror image of the advantages of being inside. Those advantages will probably cause 'euro creep' as British companies try to protect themselves by using the euro inside Britain. They will be forced to price, invoice and trade in euros with their continental trading partners. The UK has higher interest rates and may also have a volatility of interest rates which reflects these problems. That is a trading cost that increases the cost of capital which, in the long run, will have a damaging impact on the competitiveness of British industry.

Regarding the volatility of sterling against the euro, the relative size of the two markets must be considered: Euroland is five times the size of the sterling markets. Under those circumstances, the international capital markets are perfectly capable of putting a large amount of money into sterling and perhaps pushing it to excessive heights. Given the history of the bets on these currency movements, will we see sterling become a little ball on the outside of the big globe of the euro markets?

Will sterling become highly volatile? In recent years, the purchasing power parity of sterling went from about 10% cheap up to about 13-15% dear compared to its ten year average. The UK has suffered the volatile rise of sterling but what will be the economic and political consequences of a volatile decline?

Trade difficulties. One of the risks that may crystallise is protectionism. The current review of the single financial market legislation could be a threat. It may be tempting for the EU to insert clauses that have the side effect that, if the UK is not 'in' within a few years, discrimination may be possible against financial services provided from the City of London. All single market legislation is either created or amended by qualified majority voting, so the UK has no veto. If the UK attitude towards Europe and EMU is not developing in a way which its trading partners feel to be appropriate, there may be potential for further covert protectionism.

Direct Investment. The UK has gained enormously from inward investment over the past few years. More than half a million jobs have been created within the UK in the last decade. Some of the surge in UK productivity has come from inward investment of best practice from elsewhere. US companies, who are major investors in the UK, tend to ask what they should do with their investment plans if the UK remains out of EMU, and what would remaining out really mean about the UK's involvement in the European Union? Similar questions are considered by Japanese companies, some of whom have stated rather more boldly that if the UK does not join the euro within a reasonable period, there will be a real risk of inward investment drying up. There is also the added danger that UK companies, half of whose exports go to Europe, will begin to experience the same fears and decide to build new factories in Euroland rather than in the UK. So there are two sides to the investment question, the inward and the outflow.

Political Marginalisation. Another potential problem for an 'out' country is crisis management. As a hypothetical example: if East Asian and Japanese instability turns into a major crisis, what is likely to happen? Presently, the Asian debts are denominated mainly in dollars, so the US Treasury and the Fed are the main driving forces. But in future, particularly when European banks have become heavily involved, a future crisis may be partly denominated in euros. It will fall to the Council of the Eleven, and the ECB, as the issuer of the currency, to deal with that situation. Therefore, the management of the global financial system may quickly reduce from G8 down to G3 or, possibly, just G2, where the euro Eleven and the ECB deal directly with the US Treasury and the Fed.

For the UK on the outside, G2 would be a very serious blow to its self-esteem. Britain still thinks of itself as an important country, and to be excluded at the moment when its vital national interests were being debated and decided upon, would be a painful event.

For a direct or a portfolio investor the probability and timing of eventual UK entry into the single currency are crucial components of any decision to invest in sterling denominated assets. In October 1997, the Chancellor of the Exchequer laid out his basic principles for UK entry, setting out five economic tests. His key test is whether the UK economic cycle is coincident with that of Europe. If these economic tests are passed, there will be a decision on entry after the next election, followed by a decisive referendum.

The possibility of sterling entering EMU on this basic timetable is presently discounted in the gilt market. British forward interest rates approach German and French yields in about 2003. But there is still a certain risk premium, and that implies that sterling will fall to about DM 2.60-2.65, significantly down from where it is and back towards levels where British industry would be quite comfortable. This maybe what the government is hoping for: a growing feeling of inevitability that the UK will just drift in once EMU is working, followed by a smooth referendum. But there is a real risk that by adopting this 'joining by accident' policy, the UK's transition could go seriously wrong.

Would the European Union accept what many might argue to be a competitive devaluation of sterling down towards DM 2.50? The Maastricht Treaty sets out quite clearly that the final decision will be taken by the heads of government, who take account of reports from the ECB and the Commission, although they are not bound by those. Therefore, even if the UK is not in the ERM, the heads of government could still admit the UK, in accordance with the Treaty. At his nomination hearings in Brussels, Wim Duisenberg made the point specifically: 'Whatever you may say about ERM membership, currency stability is absolutely essential'. Most observers would accept that.

However, the joining by accident policy hinges on 'a settled period of convergence', to quote Chancellor Brown, and thus the absence of recession. Any need to slash interest rates, with sterling out, could generate volatile capital flows. These possibilities raise the real risk that sterling will become a very volatile currency and that currency stability for the requisite two years, or even a shorter period, will never happen. It is a risk. Simply getting inflation down to the same level as the rest of Europe does not automatically cause currency stability.

The overall danger is the UK may simply assume that, by accident or inevitability, it can get into EMU. If that is the government's central strategy, it may not work. Britain may find itself disappointed because of its previous lack of true commitment — in marked contrast to the commitment shown by Italy, Spain and Portugal in designing every policy to get into EMU. The fact is that the United Kingdom appears to be waiting for a happy coincidence. If that does not transpire, Britain may distance itself from monetary union and damage seriously its whole European relationship. Investors will pay careful attention to these developments. As the financial markets of Euroland develop, they may become an ever more attractive safe haven from any difficulties that may develop in the UK.

---

[1] The views expressed are the author's own and are not necessarily shared by Salomon Smith Barney or any of its affiliates.
[2] See Article 104a (**Article 102**): no privileged access to financial institutions.

5. EMU and Unemployment

John Monks

As of June 1998, unemployment in the fifteen EU member states was officially posted at 18 million, or 10.2% compared with 4.7% in the United States and 4.1% in Japan. These grim statistics are blamed by some on the deflationary consequences of the application of the Maastricht convergence criteria, and by others on the lack of response in European labour markets to the flexibility which those criteria require.

These points need to be addressed, but a discussion of EMU cannot be isolated from the development of the European Union in the round. The European institutional system is inclusive. It operates with checks and balances and has moved a long way towards activating through successive amendments to the Treaties the initial, social and political, as well as economic, objectives of the signatories of the Rome Treaty over 40 years ago.

So far as employment and social policy are concerned, the single market discussions were accompanied by those on the social charter and acceptance in particular of qualified majority voting on health and safety issues. The single currency decisions, logically extending the single market, were linked to the social chapter of the Treaty of Maastricht (1992), supplemented by the Employment Title of the Treaty of Amsterdam (1997). Further EU enlargement, as well as EMU, will need to bring a renewed development of democratic accountability at all levels.

Through these processes the European Union is evolving a sui generis economic and social model which is sufficiently broad and robust to cope with the challenges of a globalising economy and of technological change that can take our societies forward. This model embraces competition as well as cooperation and solidarity, and seeks to find a balance between them.

For Europe to work fully for us, we need to work fully with it. The UK has a pretty dismal record of missing the European boat and, on EMU, history is in danger of repeating itself. Some governments might not like it, but the trend towards and the necessity of an economic management of Europe growing out of the euro Eleven Council is clear, and the cost to Britain of our exclusion from it will become so increasingly.

Flexible labour markets

The first task we face is to resist the still fashionable view that deregulation and something called the 'flexible labour market' is the secret of economic success. We have to be very careful with our terms here. For flexibility is fast becoming the key word in today's economic policy debate.

But too often 'flexibility' obscures more than it illuminates. The word itself now has a flexible meaning and can hinder debate and real insight. The truth is that some things that are called flexibility can help cut unemployment, raise living standards and boost competitiveness. But there are other things that are just as often called flexibility that are a cover for backward practices that do no-one any good at all, other than the worst kind of employer. So this is not an attack on the concept of flexibility, but rather an objection to those who seek to define it as anti-employee.

Undoubtedly firms and organisations need to be flexible so that they can respond to rapid changes in market conditions. Their staff in turn need to be able to contribute fully to the firm's flexibility, but this is not the same as — and is often the opposite of — the flexibility to hire and fire at random.

The fashionable view in the 1980s, which is now staging something of a come back, is that EU labour markets are inflexible, that US labour markets are flexible and that this explains the differences in unemployment performance. This was, and still is, a caricature.

Europe is a big and diverse place and cannot be treated as having a single labour market. In fact, about 30% of the population of OECD Europe works in labour markets with long term average unemployment rates lower than those of the US. Moreover, many of those European labour markets are not noted for their light regulation. Indeed, by UK standards they tend to be much more heavily regulated, both formally and informally, through collective bargaining.

Most independent research in fact implies that the EU labour market is far from being sclerotic compared with the US. There is a great deal of job creation and destruction going on across all labour markets. Nor does research suggest that those countries with less formal employment protection do better than those with more highly regulated labour markets.

Steve Nickell has provided a good summary of those things which do not seem to have much impact on unemployment in Europe.[1] These are:

- employment protection legislation

- high labour market standards legally enforced

- high unionisation

- generous unemployment benefits.

Nevertheless, generous benefits available without a time limit and not linked to active labour market policies are thought to add to unemployment, especially long term unemployment.

Wage bargaining systems may also matter, especially the degree of wage coordination, although just how much is not clear. The OECD has recently concluded that, with the one great exception of earnings inequality, there is no strong statistical link between bargaining systems and overall economic performance.[2]

So it may be that the system matters less than the way it works in practice. Work by the OECD suggests that workers in economies regarded as lightly regulated and with a similar employment structure to the UK, such as Denmark and the Netherlands, nonetheless have much lower levels of perceived job insecurity. And job security, and the long term employment relations this encourages, is good for long term investment in human capital.

Other important work is being undertaken at the Cranfield Institute, which looks at how flexible in practice real people and real organisations are across Europe and the US. It finds that the UK comes top of only two leagues: for ease of hire and fire, and for staff who work excessively long hours.

For more important measures such as the ability of organisations to rapidly introduce new products, and for the skills of their workers, Britain's position was disappointing. It is hardly much consolation to know that managers in the UK can easily get rid of staff after they have failed to win orders.

These conclusions certainly call into question some of the wilder claims that the so called Rhineland system is dead and buried, and that wholesale dismantling of social protection and industrial relations systems is now the only solution to European unemployment. Repeating the mantra that the European model is dead does not make it true. Just imagine how the UK economy would have coped if we had suddenly had to merge with East Germany.

Britain has the biggest share of low wage employment in Europe, the biggest share of very long hour jobs, and the highest levels of job insecurity. According to DTI measures of labour market performance concerning added value and competitiveness, the UK trails the more dynamic economies of Europe. British labour productivity is 20% lower than in the US, and 25-30% lower than in France and Germany. The UK achieves less investment per worker than any other major industrial country, and we have fewer qualified people than France or Germany.

On the other hand, the kind of partnership relationships established in many of Britain's most successful firms provide a much better basis for underpinning genuine flexibility. The basic deal is normally that staff agree to be adaptable, to learn new skills and accept that change will be constant. In return employers pledge security, provide training and a chance to share in the success of the firm. That is part of a European approach to social policy.

European social policy

With the full incorporation of the social chapter into the Treaty in Amsterdam, the EU now has a powerful tool with which to lay down minimum standards in the social field. The Treaty introduces the possibility for those standards to be negotiated between European trade union and employers' organisations and then extended through a decision of the Council, thereby avoiding the traditional EU legislative procedures. This innovation contributes to subsidiarity in the correct sense of the term — although some employers will interpret the institutional innovation as an excuse to do nothing.

It is in this context that the parental leave, part-time work and fixed-term work agreements have been or are being negotiated. That is what I would call positive flexibility.

One of the great successes of European social policy has been the establishment of European Works Councils across the European Economic Area, although the TUC would have preferred it if the directive had been brought forward to cover a negotiated agreement with the European employers. There is little doubt that without the directive, employers would be considerably less willing to even talk to the unions, much less reach workable agreements. The agreements were signed and the sky did not fall — despite the predictions of British employers and the previous government about the negative effect of their introduction on competitiveness.

So, if European Works Councils have not been the ogre previously presented to the UK, and indeed have been beneficial to social partnership, why do we now have a campaign mounted against the possibility of informing and consulting workers in national companies? Britain should not be nervous about proposals for a basic right for workers to information and consultation. Why should two such simple principles be a burden on business when they are essential components of any good public or voluntary organisation?

A partnership approach to EMU

Although the UK will not join the single currency on 1 January 1999, the introduction of the euro will have a direct and immediate effect at the workplace for many British workers.

In particular, the vast majority of European Works Councils will cover companies of which either the headquarters or subsidiaries are situated in countries within the euro zone. European Works Council representatives will be among the first British trade unionists who will be affected by the introduction of the euro. There are at present more than a thousand of them, and this will increase to well over five thousand by the time all relevant companies covered by the directive have set up their European Work Council.

The TUC has developed a checklist for these key trade union opinion formers. It sets down examples of practical issues to be raised with management, and seeks to draw on the experience of trade union colleagues from the euro zone. Employers should take advantage of the forum of the European Work Council to discuss the consequences of EMU for their company. There also is a need for such discussions at the level of national companies fostered by their trade associations in cooperation with trade unions, all the more pressing given the degree of ignorance of the issues revealed by the recent Treasury survey of small and medium sized businesses.[3]

The setting up by the Chancellor of the Exchequer of the EMU standing committee and business advisory group, with TUC participation in both, were helpful steps. The decision to produce options for a national changeover plan by the end 1998 is welcome. The next step will require wider participation among the social partners.

Amsterdam employment title

In the Treaty of Amsterdam, it was agreed that member states should 'work towards developing a coordinated strategy for employment and particularly for promoting a skilled, trained and adaptable workforce and labour markets responsive to economic change'.[4] The introduction of an employment title to the Treaty and the acceptance of strengthened growth and employment policies, including intensified activity by the European Investment Bank, opens up new avenues for action so far as employment is concerned. It was a response to the demand advanced first by trade unions and by a few governments, but which eventually achieved the required unanimity thanks in particular to intervening changes of government in France and the UK, that the provisions of the Treaty dealing with policy on EMU needed a counterpoint on employment policy, including social partner involvement.

The Luxembourg jobs summit in November 1997 agreed to bring some of the Amsterdam employment provisions into effect even before the Treaty is ratified by all member states. It set down four practical and achievable jobs guidelines:

- improving employability

- developing entrepreneurship

- encouraging adaptability of businesses and their employees

- strengthening equal opportunity policies.

The policy poses challenges for the social partners who are to be involved to an unprecedented extent in the development of measures. At the same time, governments are to set specific targets to offer new starts to unemployed young people and long term unemployed adults, as well as on training, to be advanced through national employment action plans.

In the UK, the action plan was agreed in tripartite discussion, and the TUC and the CBI provided jointly drafted chapters on training and work organisation. It has been a long time since the words 'national plan' were uttered in Britain, sanctioned by government. This is an example of how the development of social dialogue in the UK is being driven by the European Union. There is nevertheless yet more progress to be made to reach the objectives of the European Trade Union Confederation, which are aimed at ensuring that the social partners are involved fully and systematically in the drawing up, implementation and monitoring of the action plans, and that equality between women and men is put into effect across all four of the employment guidelines.

The conclusions of the Cardiff European Council of June 1998 are a good step in the right direction. They recognised the importance of the contribution of the European social partners, who met the troika of the immediate past, present and next presidents of the Council on the eve of the summit, and underlined the need for economic reform to be linked to social dialogue.

The European Council carried out an initial assessment of the national employment plans and set orientations for future work on employment to include:

• developing skills and adaptability, with particular attention being paid to older workers

• strengthening action on equal opportunities through mainstreaming, and promoting family-friendly working practices

• tackling discrimination against people with disabilities, ethnic minorities and other groups disadvantaged in the labour market

• promoting new ways of organising work, where necessary by reviewing existing regulations, to combine flexibility with security

• reviewing the tax and benefit system

• developing entrepreneurship, particularly through encouraging small businesses.

Those are central approaches in the developing European model.

Action for job creation

Of course, supply-side action is not enough. As the Commission points out in its recent employment report, 'in order to produce their full return, training policies must go together with a strong creation of working posts in the economy so that people going through these re-training efforts do indeed find a job at the end of it'.[5]

Action is needed on the demand side too. The special programme of the European Investment Bank agreed in Amsterdam is to be welcomed. But the 1993 White Paper of Jacques Delors on growth, competitiveness and employment should now be revisited — and with less parsimony. The Commission's work, led by Neil Kinnock, on public-private initiatives for infrastructural projects is a way forward.

The United States has a better record than Europe on innovation, investment, and the use of venture capital, especially for small high tech firms. This, combined with the huge US market and macroeconomic stability, is what really underwrites the US success in job creation (while remembering the ghettos and the massive prison population there).

Similarly it should be remembered, even in the current difficult situation which requires a stimulation of demand, that Japan is better at process innovation and investment than the EU. In promoting economic efficiency and social progress, Europe can learn from other countries. But this must be done according to our own specificities.

In Europe, the single market and the preparations for its real completion in EMU, add to the need for us to adapt. We face even more company level, regional and economy-wide restructuring, and that could be destabilising. So proactive economic measures are needed, and they need not be in breach of the convergence criteria on public deficits and debt.

Convergence criteria flexibility

There is undoubtedly concern, not least among Europe's electors, that the application of policies designed to achieve the Maastricht convergence criteria will damage the real economy. This is a serious argument, and the issue has been high on the TUC's agenda for some time.

A key issue for the 'outs' is whether they would, in practice, be able to follow a more lax fiscal policy. However, it seems likely that pressure to reduce budget deficits will be even greater on the out countries, and that those with a deficit above 3% will pay a heavy interest rate premium. This is partly what drove Spain, Portugal and Italy so hard, and at considerable cost, to be in the first wave.

In addition, the criteria are more flexible than some would have it. The budgetary criteria, written in a Protocol to the Treaty as reference values, specifically allow for cyclical downturns. This element has featured strongly in the arguments put forward by Europe's trade unions, both individually and through the European Trade Union Confederation.

There is nothing in the Treaty which condemns participating member states to permanent deflation. EMU provides for a stable and predictable level of inflation. So long as other appropriate policies are followed, this is quite compatible with economic growth and high levels of employment. This argues for more action on employment at European level, and the TUC hopes that the Austrian and German presidencies of the Council in 1998-99 will be working in that direction. Otherwise there will be a tendency to blame every cutback in public service provision on Maastricht and EMU: from the point of view of a public service worker losing his or her job such a reaction can be understood.

The fact that as many as eleven countries passed the threshold to enter the final stages of EMU during the famous weekend of 2-3 May 1998 implies that the reference values were not applied mechanically. But the reaction of the money markets showed that they agreed that such flexibility did not call into question the soundness of the euro.

Devaluation

The fixed exchange rate of EMU will deprive the participating states of the ability to devalue. This has to be taken seriously, but it is not as straightforward as it seems.

First, it has to remembered that the euro Eleven will in any case influence the exchange rates of the 'outs'. Second, only nominal rates will be fixed under EMU, but for competitiveness what matters is the real exchange rate. Movements in the nominal rate do not always correspond with the real exchange rate. Third, devaluation is never a painless process. People in the devaluing country may not like the fact that their incomes are lower than they would otherwise have been.

It is the real economy that matters and no monetary fix, whether a fixed rate or floating rate system, can alter that fact.

It should also be borne in mind that any attempt by the UK to engage in competitive devaluation would attract a heavy reaction against the British irrespective of obligations under single market rules, and that in turn would undermine further the country's attractiveness for inward investment, which is already weakened by its non-participation in the first wave.

Exchange rate

British industry cannot afford another four or five years of exchange rate instability. Manufacturing in Britain is in recession, at least technically, mainly because of the 27% increase in sterling's nominal exchange rate since August 1996 and the 30% increase in the real exchange rate. The longer this continues, the greater is the risk of the recession spreading to other parts of the economy.

The main factors determining the level of the pound are the high levels of interest rates in the UK and the fact that it is not expected to enter EMU until 2001 at the earliest. Whether or not the UK joins ERM 2, the euro Eleven are unlikely to accept as a member any country whose currency was subject to violent swings.

Two dangers have to be avoided: the continuation of the pound at its present high level and a precipitate fall in its value which could increase inflationary pressure. To avoid the twin peaks of a high pound and high inflation, policy priority should be to steer the pound towards a target rate of DM 2.50-2.60. A lower exchange rate nearer DM 2 could lead to inflationary boom, and a continuation of rate near DM 3 could lead to bust in manufacturing. The UK must have an exchange rate policy which offers a realistic entry rate and gives it a period of stability before entry. The strict wording of the Maastricht Treaty is for two years' stability. Even if the UK is not held to that by the euro Eleven, so far it has not achieved even two weeks' stability.

If we look back, British economic policy has been knocked off course by exchange rate crises, with the economy squeezed repeatedly by high interest rates. We are in danger of repeating that again today with the willingness of the Bank of England to risk the real economy by pushing rates ever higher.

Joining EMU means that Britain could eliminate exchange rate instability for the vast bulk of the economy. The UK would enjoy lower interest rates over the medium term. It would be part of a coordinated economic policy for Europe as a whole. This is an economic prize worth having, and is in itself enough for the trade union movement to campaign for a yes vote when the time comes for a referendum.

But EMU is more than an economic objective. EMU will underwrite the best standards in the world in terms of worker and union rights, social policy, welfare and public services. Much of what Europe has achieved in this regard was put in place at the national level during the long post-war economic boom. When the boom ended with the oil shocks of the 1970s, Europe's socal model came under increasing strain, as did the welfare systems of all the developed countries.

Nevertheless, European Union countries, by comparison with the United States, have eliminated poverty from unemployment. They have generally avoided the polarisation between the affluent and a large group of 'working poor', earning low wages and relegated to urban ghettos. The post-war European economy has benefited by steadily rising productivity and real wage increases that have risen in line with productivity, raising the overall standard of living.

Those are the achievements of the European social model. We need to maintain them through change.

---

[1] Steve Nickell, 'Unemployment and Labour Market Rigidities: Europe versus North America' in *Journal of Economic Perspectives*, vol. 11, no. 3.

[2] OECD Employment Outlook, 1997.

[3] HM Treasury, *Getting Ready for the Euro*, First Report, July 1998.

[4] Article 109n (**Article 125**).

[5] European Commission, 'Growth and Employment in the Stability-Oriented Framework of EMU', *Economic policy reflections in view of the forthcoming 1998 Broad Guidelines*, 1998.

6. Making EMU Work

David Currie

The launch of the euro on 1 January 1999 comes at an especially critical time for the European and world economies. Only a year ago the timing seemed particularly benign, with the European economy moving into upswing after a period of depressed growth and with inflation nonexistent. At that time, the storm clouds in Asia seemed rather a remote threat. But now with continuing and deepening problems in Japan and the rest of Asia, with deep crisis in Russia, and contagion spreading to Latin America and Central Europe, the global context for the launch of the euro looks more threatening.

This worsened global context is not a reason for questioning the euro project. Indeed what has been notable about the tornado that has swept through world currency markets is that it has so far left unscathed the eleven euro member states. Countries that would hitherto have been swept up in the turmoil have been grateful for the protection afforded by the prospective launch of the euro. But the global context does place a premium on making the euro work well. Instability emanating from Western Europe as a result of problems with the launch of the euro or with its subsequent operation could help to tip the world economy into deeper recession and a more difficult recovery. Making the euro work well is not just in the interests of the euro Eleven, and the later entrants, including the UK, but also of the US, Japan and the rest of the world.

The euro Eleven have already made impressive adjustments to get to where they are now. Few would have predicted five years ago the degree of fiscal consolidation achieved as a result of the Maastricht convergence process in those countries that in the past have not enjoyed stable fiscal and monetary policies. The degree of convergence that has been achieved is impressive. But having said that, it is important to emphasise that now is not a time to relax. Whether the euro works well depends very much on how policy is conducted from now on. It is by no means determined and it is policies from now over the next two to five years that will decide whether the euro works well and the European economy is strong, or whether it proves to be a rather mixed blessing. European policy-makers have it in their hands to determine the outcome.

The benefits of the euro

What will the euro mean? From the point of view of business, one of the key things that the euro will bring is an increasingly open and transparent market across the European economy. This will lead to much greater competition, in effect allowing the real completion of the whole single market project. From that perspective, it is nothing startlingly new, but simply a continuation of the progressive integration of the European economy that we have seen since the Single European Act and before. The single currency represents a key further step in that direction.

It is worth comparing the European economy with the United States, where we see a very vibrant, highly competitive market of a similar (marginally smaller) size, with prices very significantly lower than in Europe. These benefits, to American consumers and firms alike, arise from the depth, transparency and openness of the US market place, allowing greater integration and efficiency and therefore much greater economies of scale and scope. This would not be possible without the single currency that the dollar represents.

Similarly, the deep integration project on which Europe is embarked is feasible only with a single currency. The single currency eliminates all exchange rate risk. People will often say: 'well, of course, you can hedge against exchange rate risk', and that is perfectly true. But if one is building a factory with a life of 20 or 25 years, it does not make sense to hedge the exposure of the factory over that length of time, because exposure to a whole set of other risks would also rise, increasing the overall riskiness of the business. So the principal advantage of the single currency is that it eliminates exchange rate risk, thereby eliminating the exchange rate influence on location and sourcing decisions. As a result, we will see significant rationalisation of industry to the long run benefit of the European economy.

For many countries, another advantage of the single currency, backed as it is by the European Central Bank, will be that it will give much greater assurance of price stability. This is something that matters for those countries such as Italy, Portugal, Spain and the UK, which in the past have experienced high inflation. There is a much greater assurance of low inflation; and I suspect we will see the benefits that flow from that appearing quite quickly.

What the euro means for business

The launch of the euro represents a major development for companies, requiring them to think through all aspects of operations and strategy. Typically, companies started to adapt to EMU by thinking of the nuts and bolts questions: what the euro means for IT and accountancy systems, and for legal contracts. They then woke up to the implications for pricing and the fact that the greater transparency brought by the euro will make it much less easy to discriminate between different national markets. Then they moved on to thinking about their branding strategy and the need to replace national with European brands. Now companies are also thinking through the consequences of human resource policy. Most importantly, the best companies are reassessing their entire strategy, recognising that the greater integration of the European markets will affect their positioning in it and their competitive advantage. This process of rethinking the business from top to bottom will yield much more competitive industries. Getting the process right is the key contribution that business must make to ensuring that the euro works. The companies that gain most will be those that are ahead of the curve in rethinking their strategic positioning.

This process means, of course, transitional adjustment costs, with losers as well as gainers. The challenge is to manage the transition so as to secure long-term advantage. That requires imagination and flexibility by both business and policy-makers. Provided that the ECB can sustain Europe's recovery, despite the turmoil in other parts of the world, then the restructuring associated with the euro need not be too painful: a fairly buoyant European economy will make the required restructuring that much easier to accomplish. The prize to be won is the longer run benefit of greater efficiency and higher living standards, to the benefit of consumers and firms alike.

Demand side risks of the euro

What are the risks? These can be divided into two main categories. There are the risks on the demand side, concerning the conduct of euro monetary and fiscal policy within EMU. And there are the risks on the supply side, arising from inflexibility of product and labour markets in the euro-zone.

On the demand side, one can imagine a number of factors going wrong, or not going as well as they should. The European Central Bank has a pretty tough job of running monetary policy through the next few years in a period in which all our money holding patterns are likely to shift. We will find ourselves moving both the location and denomination of bank accounts. It is very likely that with the adoption of the euro will come a money demand shift of the kind that we saw in the UK and in the US in the early 1980s associated with financial liberalisation and leading to monetary policy errors. This will make it much harder for the ECB to conduct euro monetary policy. The indicators of monetary policy will be difficult for the ECB to interpret. Despite the very experienced Executive Board chosen for the ECB, we have the risk of monetary policy errors during the settling down period for the euro.

A more serious deep-set risk arises from the possibility of conflict between the European Central Bank and the finance ministers. The potential for real conflict will occur if finance ministers think that, having reduced their fiscal deficits to get under the wire of the 3% Maastricht convergence criteria, they can now relax and allow fiscal deficits to rise again. The risk of conflict is more likely to materialise if the European economy proves more stagnant, and if supply side reforms are not carried out. If euro fiscal policy is indeed relaxed, then larger fiscal deficits could lead to the ECB maintaining a rather tight monetary policy. This policy combination could easily result in a volatile and overvalued euro. Just as the dollar was volatile and overvalued in the 1980s with Reagonomics (the combination of a large fiscal deficit and a tight monetary policy), one may fear the same policy mix emerging twenty years later on the European side of the Atlantic.

The Stability Pact provides significant constraints on the conduct of fiscal policy, limiting its relaxation and providing for fines for those countries that step out of line. But the sceptic can point to the difficulty that could arise were a large number of states to relax fiscal policy, since it is not obvious that states will vote to fine each other if they are all in the same position of having broken the Pact.

The opposite danger is that fiscal stabilisers may not be allowed to operate as a result of the Stability Pact. The Stability Pact confines fiscal deficit to a ceiling of 3% of GDP, unless there is a very severe recession. But it would be desirable to allow the deficit to rise and fall with the cycle, rising in periods of depressed demand and falling in periods of high demand, allowing automatic fiscal stabilisers to operate to moderate the cycle. The need for automatic stabilisers is enhanced by the lack of flexibility in monetary policy at the national level, and without them the macroeconomic cycle at the national level could well be much bumpier. With world recession a clear risk, this is not a remote concern.

On the one hand, therefore, it is desirable that fiscal stabilisers should be allowed to operate, while, on the other, high deficits should be avoided. How does one resolve this dilemma? The answer is that member state governments should be aiming at a fiscal deficit target, in accordance with the Stability Pact, of a budget balanced on average over the cycle (perhaps in the 0-1% range as a percentage of GDP), rather than at the 3% or a little under that many have achieved to date. That would allow the fiscal deficit to rise in periods of recession without breaching the Stability Pact, so that stabilisation policy through automatic fiscal stabilisers could operate at the national level. This requires a further effort to be made by governments to lower, and indeed eliminate, structural deficits. It is therefore crucial that governments continue the process of fiscal consolidation over the next year or two if European expansion is sustained, so that when the next European slowdown begins fiscal policy is in a position to respond.

Supply side risks

Europe's supply side flexibility needs to be enhanced. The launch of the euro means the loss of the tool of exchange rate flexibility. The loss is not that great, since exchange rate flexibility has all too often been misused. But we need to develop the flexibility of the European market in order to avoid undue supply side rigidity and consequent unemployment. Unemployment is already high in many parts of Europe, and it is crucial to avoid exacerbating the problem through excessive rigidities in labour and product markets, since this would be deeply worrying for the future of the EMU.

A key feature of the European economy is that Europeans do not move very much. They do not move very much even within their own national borders, but they are certainly disinclined to move across borders, partly because of language but also for other cultural and economic reasons. That makes many Americans sceptical about whether EMU can work; they note that Europe does not have in place a system of fiscal transfers between countries in the euro-zone, in the way that the Federal taxation system provides in the US. With no inter-country transfers and low labour mobility, they reasonably ask how adjustment to country-specific shocks will occur.

The answer is that Europe needs to ensure that its labour and products markets are flexible enough to allow for such adjustment. This implies reform of our labour market institutions, the opening up of our product markets, and the promotion of entrepreneurship and risk-taking. All of this is needed so that, when jobs have to disappear as they inevitably must in a dynamic market economy, there are a variety of adjustments mechanisms available. People could, in extreme circumstances, take lower wages as a way of keeping employment. They would also have the opportunity to move into new jobs in other sectors, and possibly new sectors, that are created in dynamic, entrepreneurial product markets. This labour and product market dynamism needs to combine with an active labour market of training and skills, getting the educational and training component of labour market policies right.

A key point is that there are many different ways of achieving this supply side flexibility, and that there is no single, correct model. There is the British/US model of a rather deregulated labour market, and there are the examples of continental European economies that have a rather more centralised labour market model but which use this centralised feature to deliver wage adjustment and flexibility. Other models are available. This is an issue on which subsidiarity should obtain: we certainly do not need a common labour market policy laid down from Brussels.

But appealing to subsidiarity does not mean that any model will do. It must be one that delivers flexibility, and not all countries in Europe seem to have learnt that lesson. In particular, the move to limiting working hours as a way of tackling high unemployment seems to be moving in exactly the wrong direction. If Euroland countries were not to adopt the flexibility agenda, then the risks from EMU will increase, and the euro will work less well.

Making the euro work well requires us to combine all these elements. Business must respond to the launch of the euro by appropriate strategic responses to derive maximum benefit, while governments must put in place effective demand side and flexible supply side policies.

Issues of governance

There is another, deeper question for the European Union that is posed by its prospective enlargement, and which also bears on issues raised by the euro. Enlargement is fundamental to the development of the EU, and the Union has shown some weakness in not addressing this issue earlier and more effectively. But with enlargement the EU will have to face the key issue of governance. The truth of the matter is that the rules that were devised for the original six, which are now creaking with fifteen, will clearly not work with twenty-five member states in the European Union. And that issue is a fundamental one, for EMU initiates the first institution in the Union devised for a subset of member states, namely the ECB governed by the countries of Euroland. The Council of the euro Eleven, which has an influential part to play in the role of overseeing the Stability Pact and the operation of fiscal policy in EMU, is also an emerging body that will become more important. I think that this represents the logical development of the Union in a direction that allows it to combine in a manageable way the dual agenda that has driven the EU from its inception: the deepening agenda, currently represented by the euro, and the strategic, widening agenda represented by enlargement. The EU may well have to evolve towards a dual structure with two elements: first, a group of countries committed to the full integration menu, table-d'hôte, fixed price; and a second group who, whether from necessity or choice, prefer the à la carte, pick'n'mix approach. The second group would have to accept rather less influence over the overall direction of the EU.

The EU has tended to duck these issues of governance, but their resolution is a key longer-term element in making the euro work well. With ineffective governance structures, the euro will not realise its full potential.

Alternative scenarios

Let me paint alternative scenarios of how EMU may work over the next ten years. Scenarios are not forecasts of what is to happen, but, rather, they highlight possibilities. I emphasise that because at least one of my scenarios is a rather unpleasant one. I do not want to be interpreted as saying 'this will happen', for I believe that European policy-makers are sensible enough to avert it. The purpose of setting it out as a possibility is to highlight the importance of guarding against these risks. The scenarios have two dimensions of policy: the first is aimed at policy makers and says 'this is what you have to get right in order to make this new venture work, and if you do not, this is the consequence'; the second, aimed at the rest of us, is meant to put pressure on governments to deliver. I have alluded to the two dimensions already, namely, first getting the demand side right (that is, conducting monetary policy well, aiming for low fiscal deficits of 0-1%, and then allowing fiscal stabilisers to operate), and, second, achieving supply side flexibility (that is, flexible labour and product markets, enhanced skills and entrepreneurship).

These two dimensions give rise to four scenarios. The first is of a nightmare Europe in decline, both stagnant and volatile. Consider the possibility of unstable demand policies, with the European Central Bank making mistakes in the early years of the launch of the euro, combined with finance ministers permitting lax fiscal policies. In the worst case, this could result in major conflict between the ECB and national governments, possibly even new governments that had no say in the choice of those sitting on the ECB. There would then be a question of legitimacy between elected representatives and an appointed ECB.

Such conflicts can more easily arise against the background of high unemployment, particularly if policy is not such as to promote jobs and reduce unemployment. Conflicts between policy authorities may then lead to jumpiness in forex markets, generating an unstable euro. Together with volatile interest rates, this could well reinforce high unemployment and a stagnant European economy. Put that together with an ageing population in Europe and a rising dependency ratio, and the consequent need to fund unfunded pension liabilities in the public sector, and public finances would come under intense pressure. However determined were the actions of finance ministers to keep deficits within the Stability Pact, against this background fiscal deficits could well rise, and the unpopularity of the resulting forced fiscal retrenchments could give rise to growing discontent across Euroland. If that happened, politicians would be quite likely to look for somebody on whom to deflect criticism and those sitting in Frankfurt would provide a clear, natural target. One can imagine growing disenchantment with the adoption of the euro, calls for the restoration of national currencies and the rise of extreme, nationalist parties.

This represents an unpleasant and dangerous scenario which could lead to the break-up of the EU and the Single Market. So if the euro fails to be made to work, if policy is got wrong, the EU will be weakened rather than strengthened, and even its existence threatened. I believe that the chances of this are quite small, but averting it requires the right policy responses, as well as a wide appreciation of the risks that this scenario highlights.

Now suppose that policy makers, both central bankers and finance ministers, conduct policy in a broadly sensible way, but the need for supply side flexibility is neglected. This would result in a much more stable macroeconomic environment, which is helpful. Provided that Asian flu does not prove too virulent, we may continue to enjoy a good phase of recovery from recession, with falling unemployment. But if, in that period, the opportunity is not taken to advance flexibility by putting in place the reforms required to make labour and product markets work better, we may well find that the growth phase is rather transitory. Europe could settle back to low growth rates, inflationary pressures could re-emerge and the ECB would be forced to offset these pressures with high interest rates. This points to a scenario without major instabilities, but with a rather slumbering, sluggish European economy, weak growth and a lack of vitality. After all the hype surrounding the euro launch, that would be a disappointment.

A rather better scenario would be where demand side policy works badly, so that interest rate and exchange rate instabilities appear, but nonetheless the politicians push ahead on the flexibility agenda. That would imply volatile change, and, despite the instabilities, a Europe that is adjusting and dynamic. One could imagine the conflict between monetary and fiscal policy alluded to above, with consequent euro instability. But with supply side reforms, the long run trend of unemployment could be downwards, Europe's competitiveness could be enhanced and it could, in the long run, grow more rapidly than it has over the last decade, despite short run instabilities.

Finally there is the rosy scenario in which European policy-makers get both arms of policy right, and the European economy does very well. Demand policies are stable, and policies to enhance supply side flexibility are put in place. The result is a dynamic European economy that generates low unemployment and can confidently extend to the East without concerns over employment in the West: Europe is revitalised. That, of course, is the scenario that all of us would like to see happen; I judge that it is also the more likely, not least because a large amount of political capital is invested in the success of the euro, so that failure is very costly. However, this favourable outcome is not preordained, and its realisation depends crucially on what we do over the next few years.

So to summarise, there are two major issues that must be addressed. The first is the need to make the euro work well, and I have emphasised the two key dimensions of demand side policy and supply side policy. Unlike a Greek tragedy, there is nothing inevitable and predetermined in all this: the future lies in our hands and we can determine and shape it for good or ill.

The second big issue is the long-run shape of the Europe that we are creating, an issue that in the UK often goes under the heading of the 'F-word', federation — or, indeed, the 'double F-word', fear of federation. This is the fundamental question, which the British are reluctant to address, about the nature of the governance of the European Union. In many respects, Europe is already an embryonic federation with large swathes of national law subject to European law, and with decisions made in Brussels — and Frankfurt — about things that affect us all. It would be better to face up to reality, and accept that the proper debate is about the nature of the federation that is evolving: heavy-handed and centralised versus light-handed and devolved. After the launch of the euro, the challenge to which Europe must rise is that of creating a genuinely democratic, devolved governance structure that can face the demands of the next century.

7. Britain's Membership

Christopher Johnson

British Prime Ministers sometimes profess an ambition to transform Britain's relations with the continent of Europe, but what the late Harold Macmillan called 'events' blow them off course in mid-Channel, and they may end up back at their starting point. The continental countries welcome Britain's contribution to Europe, but the British have always had an 'offshore' mentality. British involvement in Europe since the war has been too little, too late. History may be about to repeat itself in the case of the single currency. Now that the euro is going ahead with 11 out of 15 European Union countries, Britain faces the challenge of making up for lost time by joining EMU within a few years. Better late than never.

There is a political case for the single currency, but the economic case stands on its own. Economic and monetary union need not mean political union as well, although it provides a political framework for the peaceful settlement of economic and monetary differences.

British business as reported by the CBI is about three to one in favour of the single currency, and is not well represented by a vocal minority of dissident chairmen. Small firms and the City of London are divided more or less down the middle. Public opinion was two to one against, but is moving in favour. The pound is seen by some as a national symbol, a feature peculiar to the UK within Europe, where others see national currencies as a barbaric relic. Opinion could change if the 'New Labour' government can convince itself and the voters that the economic advantages of a successful single currency will be substantial.

ECONOMIC BENEFITS

More trade in the single market

Lower cross-border transaction costs are an obvious advantage of the single currency, with a saving of about 0.3% of GDP. The percentage saving will be bigger for tourists and small firms than for large companies. Banks in the UK will need to spend at least £900 m converting to the new currency, and the costs for the whole economy could be about £2.5 bn, also 0.3% of GDP, but these will be once-for-all, while the transactions savings will be permanent. The conversion costs will be spent within the UK economy, so will not be a loss to GDP.

The single market will not yield its full potential without the single currency, which will lead to an increase in UK trade with Europe worth far more than the transaction cost savings. Exchange rates are a major non-tariff barrier, and their abolition within the EU should have a similar effect to price cuts in stimulating trade. The UK's exports to the rest of the EU are as large in absolute value as those of France and Italy; the difference is that the UK exports more to the rest of the world than they do. The UK exports as high a percentage of GDP as Germany both inside and outside the EU, although smaller amounts, as Germany has a higher GDP (see Table One). The euro will also increase cross-border competition and take-overs in the single market. Existing price differentials will converge downwards once prices are all quoted in the same currency.

TABLE ONE

EU Exports of Goods and GDP 1995

	GDP	Exports intra EU		Exports extra EU		Total exports	
	bn PPS	% GDP	bn PPS	% GDP	bn PPS	% GDP	bn PPS
France	1075	11.6	125	6.7	72	18.3	197
Germany	1543	12.3	190	9.0	139	21.3	329
Italy	1038	11.6	120	6.7	70	18.3	190
UK	997	12.2	122	9.1	91	21.3	212
EU	6441	14.9	960	8.8	567	23.7	1527

Note: PPS are units of purchasing power. For the EU as a whole, 1 PPS = 1 ecu.

Source: European Economy No. 63

The share of the EU in the UK's trade in services and investment income is 41%, less than the 56% share of its trade in goods (see Table Two). This explains the greater enthusiasm in manufacturing than in the City or in retailing for UK membership of the euro. It also shows that services and finance have been more protected on the continent while barriers to trade in goods have been dismantled. The UK may thus have bigger gains to make when the barriers in services and finance are in their turn removed.

TABLE TWO

EU Share in UK Payments 1997

	EU as % of world payments
Goods	56
Services	41
Investment income	41
Transfers	67
Total	50

Note: Payments are the average of credits and debits.

Source: UK Pink Book

Faster economic growth

A major boost to economic growth should come from lower interest rates, due to the elimination of the risk premium on separate currencies, and the reduction in budget deficits under the Maastricht rules. British base rates at the time of writing are 7.5%, while those for the euro are likely to be around 4%. Membership of EMU would also make economic growth more stable, by breaking the British curse of 'stop-go'. The ECB could not raise interest rates above the level needed by EMU as a whole just to suit the UK if it wanted higher rates. The Chancellor would instead have to use fiscal policy more actively, and take back control of the economy from the Bank of England.

The single currency will speed the integration of the single financial market. Bond markets in euro will integrate faster than banking markets, where domestic relationship banking is stronger. The greater size of the euro bond market, the more liquidity will improve and spreads be cut, especially for corporate borrowers. Bonds will thus gain market share at the expense of banks in the corporate market, and fixed against floating loan contracts. The integration of equity markets will take longer, but the July 1998 agreement between the London and Frankfurt stock exchanges was an important first step.

Lower interest rates will mean more business investment, more jobs, and lower mortgage rates, raising the rate of economic growth by about 0.5% a year for some years, and perhaps 0.25% permanently. Temporarily high British interest rates, far from being a reason for staying out, are a reason for going in so as to get them down.

Lower inflation

Lower inflation is a major aim of the single currency, as well as a criterion for entry. Low inflation encourages personal saving, and reduces the front-end burden of borrowing. A reduction in the nominal as well as the real interest rate due to lower inflation will be a further stimulus to investment in long-run projects. It will lower the discount rate and lengthen payback periods, as long as industry also reduces its excessively high required returns.

The UK's poor inflation record improved for a short time in 1992-96, but the pound fell by 80% against the DM in the previous thirty years. The present degree of independence of the Bank of England does not have the credibility that the new European Central Bank will have. The Bank of England has to work to an inflation target set by the Treasury, and has to take the blame for failures of monetary policy when the fault may be with the Treasury for inadequate fiscal policy. Britain, like the euro Eleven already, would gain from the greater financial credibility of the ECB.

Costs of giving up the national currency

The cost of joining the single currency is that of giving up an independent interest rate and exchange rate policy, and thus the freedom to use the ultimate weapons of devaluation or revaluation. Yet monetary autonomy is an illusion, because national authorities can fix only the interest rate, but not the exchange rate, which is also part of monetary conditions. The Bank of England may set the interest rate, but the financial markets set the exchange rate. No one country can achieve independent monetary objectives in a world of free capital flows, with the exception of the US. So monetary policy is an unguided missile. Governments cannot set and maintain any chosen rate of exchange.

Devaluation is sometimes useful to regain competitiveness and reduce unemployment, but it works only if it affects output more than prices, and that is usually in the short run if at all. Devaluation is more a symptom of failure than a recipe for success. In EMU, companies have to work directly on improving productivity in order to remain competitive, and can no longer rely on devaluation to bail them out. Similarly, revaluation can slow down an overheated economy by damping demand in export markets and forcing lay-offs, but at a high cost in terms of recession and lost output. Companies find it difficult in the short-run to make up for the sudden loss in competitiveness due to the high pound by means of a step-change in productivity.

The single market aims to make the EU an optimum currency area, so arguments about whether it already is one are beside the point. Capital movements are free in the EU, one test of an optimum currency area. The EU is better off without high mobility of labour, another test of an optimum currency area. If labour is relatively immobile, it is easier to maintain wage differentials between countries to reflect competitiveness. As countries become more integrated, the single currency brings greater advantages, and the cost of giving up separate exchange rates is reduced.

PROSPECTS FOR UK MEMBERSHIP

The second wave after 2002

EMU begins on time on 1 January 1999, with 11 out of 15 member states joining in the first wave. The remarkable achievement in tackling government deficits and debts has been derived from the will to create a closer political as well as economic union. The economic recovery under way on the European continent is also helping to push deficits down to or below the 3% mark. The other criteria, for inflation, long-term interest rates, and exchange rate stability have been more easily achieved. There has been convergence, not only of statistics, but of competence in carrying out sound, if sometimes unpopular, economic policies.

Of the four countries not joining in the first wave, Denmark is prevented only by political and Greece only by economic factors. Sweden and the UK show a mixture of the two: both are reluctant to give up sovereignty over their currencies, and neither has joined the Exchange Rate Mechanism, or indeed met the currency stability criterion on any other definition. The four second wave countries are poised between being simply 'out' or 'pre-in'.

Gordon Brown, Chancellor of the Exchequer, did not succeed in sweeping away all the uncertainties about the British government's position on EMU in his statement to the House of Commons on 27 October 1997. As in the famous Echternach Dance, he took two steps forwards and one step back. The two steps forwards were to accept the principle of a successful single currency as a benefit to Britain, and to declare that there was no constitutional obstacle to pooling monetary sovereignty. The step backwards was to say that it was impossible that the UK could join in the first wave, and improbable in the life of the present parliament. Given that the next general election may be after four years rather than five, in 2001, then 2002 appears to be the earliest possible entry date.

Mr Brown's five economic tests

Mr Brown set out five economic tests of whether the single currency will be to Britain's economic advantage, which were accompanied by a detailed Treasury assessment, *UK Membership of the Single Currency*, in October 1997, referred to as the 'Brown Paper'.

1. *Cyclical convergence*. Convergence of interest rates must occur when the UK joins, because there will be a single monetary policy. It could clearly be disruptive if rates are too far apart. British short-term rates are now 7.5%, compared with expected euro rates of 4%. Even if these rates converge by about 2000, as some believe, Mr Brown wants a period of stability to demonstrate that the convergence is sustainable. This could be postponed if rates diverge further, and it could take until 2002 before the period of stability begins. The Bank of England's remit to reduce inflation to 2.5%, if necessary by raising interest rates still further, gives no place to achievement of convergence with euro rates or to the stabilisation of the pound against the euro.

2. *Flexibility of products, wages and employment*. The rest of the EU has been lectured by the UK on the need for more labour market flexibility if EMU is to work properly. It is surprising, in view of the UK's advocacy of flexibility to its supposedly less flexible continental partners, that the Treasury judges the British economy to be as yet insufficiently flexible to meet the challenge of the single currency. Skills shortages and the consequent excessive pay increases are two aspects of the UK's lack of

flexibility. Proposed remedies include better skills training and moving more people from welfare to work under the 'new deal'.

3. *Investment.* If EMU is successful, British companies are expected to invest more because of lower interest rates and an improvement in the single market. If the UK stays out of the euro, foreign investment could in the long run be diverted to other countries. This test is already a positive encouragement to the UK to join. Both capital expenditure and the stock market will benefit from the lower interest rates that EMU will bring. Foreign direct investment will not be withdrawn if the UK stays out, but the euro area will get a bigger share of new investment, while the UK will get a bigger share if it goes in.

4. *Financial services and the City of London.* The City expects to benefit from the euro whether Britain is in or out, but the benefits will be greater if Britain is in. This test is also positive, though not decisive. The City is using the euro as a wholesale currency from the beginning of 1999, under the guidance of the Bank of England. The Bank is running an international campaign to present London as the leading financial centre for the euro, from offshore. It will face tough competition from the new onshore markets. The financial system as a whole does not expect the euro to become the UK domestic currency until early in the 21st century, and cannot even be certain of that. There will thus be the problem of running the euro and the pound as dual currencies fluctuating against each other, which other countries in EMU will not have. Only if the UK goes in will the City realise its full potential as a European financial centre, and the euro its full potential as a new world currency.

5. *Growth, stability and jobs.* The UK's present unemployment rate of just over 5% is hardly a barrier to joining EMU, even if it rises as the economy slows down. The question is whether EMU will generate the extra growth in the economy to increase the quantity and quality of jobs. The Treasury concludes that this will take some years because the convergence and flexibility tests are not yet satisfied. The flexibility concept is overworked, however. The UK has more people working longer hours with lower productivity and lower pay. Its richer EU rivals have fewer people working shorter hours with higher productivity and higher pay.

The net result is that two-thirds of EU countries have higher living standards and can afford better welfare than the UK. High unemployment in the rest of the EU is coming down thanks to the recovery. But it is up to other countries to choose their unemployment rates by the way they organise their welfare-work arrangements. If the UK can meet whatever are the right membership criteria, it should not try, and fail, to impose new criteria on other members.

Exchange rate stability

It is not clear how Mr Brown interprets the Maastricht exchange rate stability criteria. There is no support in British business for entering EMU at a high exchange rate. A rate of DM 2.50 is seen as more viable, and may well occur if UK interest rates converge downwards. The pound has to come down before it can become stable. Mr Brown has announced that Britain does not intend to re-enter the Exchange Rate Mechanism. The Treasury interprets the Maastricht Treaty to mean that the pound should stay within the normal fluctuation margins of the ERM without necessarily being inside it. If these margins are taken to be 15%, then the criterion is not difficult to pass. In practice, once interest rates converge, the exchange rate of the pound could be stabilised much closer to a new central parity.

Mr Brown should set a central rate at which the UK will join EMU, in the region of DM 2.50, or euro 1.25. This will help the pound to fall some of the way. The two years of exchange rate stability required to join EMU could then begin. According to the European Commission's ruling allowing Ireland into the euro, deviations above the central exchange rate do not matter, only deviations below it. The UK could thus spend two years edging interest rates and the pound down towards euro 1.25, and pass the exchange rate criterion for joining EMU. The Government could lock in by rejoining the ERM at that rate just before entry, and get support from the ECB to avoid overshooting below it.

Business would have a focus for expectations, and avoid the unappealing scenario of being locked into EMU at DM 2.80 or higher and facing years of slow growth. A lower rate is needed to offset the recent cost rises and stagnant productivity.

Uncertainty about timing

The UK is thus keeping its options open, while excluding the membership option for some years. Yet Mr Brown is asking business to start preparing for the euro so as to be ready to join early in the next parliament. His speech to the Confederation of British Industry on 10 November 1997 went further, indicating that companies would be able to use the euro to draw up accounts, issue shares, pay taxes, and carry out domestic money transfers. A national changeover plan to the euro for business is to be announced at the end of 1998, but still without any decision as to when or whether it is to be carried out.

Some companies wonder whether investment in preparations is justified when they still do not know whether the UK will enter. Others believe that they will have to use the euro whether or not Britain joins, and that momentum will build up for going in. A number of leading companies, such as ICI and Marks & Spencer, have announced that they will start using the euro from 1 January 1999 to satisfy the needs of their foreign customers. They see the euro as giving them a competitive edge over their rivals. Indeed, companies which continue to use the pound in their trade with Euroland will be expected to quote lower prices, to compensate their customers for having to take on the exchange rate risk of fluctuations between the euro and sterling.

One possible scenario is that the Government brings the next election forward to 2001, and wins on a pro-European platform. The decision to go in would have to be made in 2000, giving EMU just over a year to demonstrate a successful start. It could then quickly get the approval of parliament and a popular referendum for entry in 2002, when the new euro notes and coins are introduced into Euroland.

This would bring the UK to the same point sometime in 2002 as the first Eleven reached at the beginning of 1999, facing a transition period when the pound is locked to the euro, which will be available only as bank and card money. Intensive planning is already going on to see how euro notes and coins could be introduced into the UK within less than the three to three and a half years required by the first wave of countries. The UK's earliest date for full replacement of the pound by the euro is likely to be sometime in 2003 or 2004.

Mr Blair will try to convert Mr Rupert Murdoch, the proprietor of the popular *Sun* newspaper, even though it has recently reaffirmed its hostility to the euro by asking whether Mr Blair was 'the most dangerous man in Britain'. Mr Murdoch may already feel that his image as an international business leader could suffer if he is too closely identified with the Conservative leadership under William Hague. For the first time, the Conservatives are isolated from the majority of their traditional business supporters, because they have ruled out joining the euro for two parliaments. The Labour government has shown that it can work with business. It is a partnership which could get Britain into EMU with a delay of no more than three years after the start.

THE CONVERGENCE TEST

Growth divergences do not matter

Mr Brown's most important test is that the business cycles of the UK and other EU countries should converge. The test is 'whether there can be sustainable convergence between Britain and the economies of a single currency'. 'Are business cycles and economic structures compatible so that we and others could live comfortably with euro interest rates on a permanent basis?' The test requires 'a settled period of convergence'. 'The UK needs a period of economic stability to demonstrate that convergence is sustainable'.

As it stands, the Chancellor's premise — that all EMU members should have roughly the same rate of economic growth at the same time — is a false one. Not all regions of the USA have the same growth rate, certainly not in the short-term, nor do they need to. It would indeed be desirable on grounds of inter-regional equity if the UK, Ireland, Spain and Portugal were to grow faster than richer EU members. Growth rates in the EU vary among countries, but without bringing into question the sustainability either of the present degree of interest and exchange rate convergence or of EMU itself. Ireland grew by 10% in 1997, Italy by 1.5%. Arguably growth rates should not be completely synchronised, or inflationary booms will develop. Stability is helped if countries in an area are slightly out of phase with each other.

In a fully functioning single market with a single currency, growth divergences will matter even less than they do today. Countries where demand is growing faster will be able to increase their trade deficits by importing from other countries in the area, thus providing a stimulus to slower growing countries and avoiding domestic inflationary pressure. The deficits will be financed on capital account, all the more readily in the absence of exchange rate risk. Either long-term investment, or short-term banking flows will restore balance between countries, as they already do between regions in one country.

Interest rates must converge

With a single monetary policy for all, it is a tautology that interest rates will converge. In fact, long term interest rates — a Maastricht criterion, as short-term rates are not — have already converged to a much greater degree, well within the 2% spread laid down in the Treaty. French and German ten-year government bonds yielded 4.7% in summer 1998, British gilts 5.9%, and bonds of other euro countries showed much smaller spreads over French and German rates. Long-term rates are as important as short-term in assessing convergence.

The business cycle is not an act of God. The UK can assist short-term interest rate convergence, and get its exchange rate down, by means of tougher fiscal policy. In May 1997 it could have closed the current account budget deficit with tax increases of no more than £5.5 bn, about 0.65% of GDP. The right policy mix required lower interest rates and higher taxes to help business and curb the consumer. However, according to the Treasury Brown Paper: 'Some would say that if the UK were to join EMU in the first wave interest rates would be lower than those required for price stability in the UK. They go on to say that fiscal policy might have to be tightened excessively to offset the ensuing demand pressures'. This curious use of 'some' has been taken to refer to Mr Brown's neighbour in Downing Street, Mr Blair, who has been unwilling to jeopardise both his enormous popularity and his election pledges by putting up taxes on consumers.

The case for singling out the UK, as the Treasury says, is that if interest rates were too low to ensure price stability in the UK, fiscal policy would have to be tightened. This is exactly what is envisaged under EMU. If countries no longer have independent monetary policy, they will have to use fiscal policy to manage demand in their economies. The policy mix will have to be shifted towards looser monetary and tighter fiscal policy, as has been happening to varying degrees in the EU as countries have striven to meet the Maastricht excessive deficit criterion.

Now that monetary policy has been tightened, the question is how soon can it be loosened to prevent the economy slowing down too quickly, without change in fiscal policy. This question has lost some of its urgency given that the possibility of EMU entry is no longer imminent. However, if the Chancellor wants a period of stable convergence before joining, the sooner the policy mix is adjusted towards looser monetary policy, the sooner that period can begin from a point where interest rates and the exchange rate can be set at levels sustainable after UK entry.

Fiscal stability needed

A reason for a tight fiscal policy is that the EU Growth and Stability Pact enjoins countries to aim at budget balance in a normal year, so as to allow the automatic stabilisers to move the budget into deficit in response to shocks yet remain within the 3% deficit limit. The government's aim is to come close to budget balance, but it could be argued that a budget surplus is the correct response to a situation of excessive growth, if balance is to be achieved in a normal year (see Table Three). If the economy slows down more than expected in response to higher interest rates, the deficit could increase again.

The Treasury analysis makes it look as if convergence is likely to occur only momentarily, and it is hard to see how a period of stability could occur if the UK economy continues to be managed independently of the euro area. It is as if one had to go on getting the same lucky numbers time after time in order to win a lottery. The UK can win only by stacking the odds in its favour, in other words by locking fiscal and monetary policy to that of the euro Eleven once interest rate convergence is achieved, and forgetting about convergence of growth rates.

TABLE THREE

UK Budget Plans and Maastricht

Percentages of GDP

	1997-98	1998-99	1999-00	2000-01	2001-02	Average
Current surplus	0.3	0.8	0.7	1.0	1.3	0.8
Net investment	0.8	0.8	1.0	1.2	1.4	1.0
Public net borrowing	0.4	0.0	0.3	0.2	0.1	0.2
Net public debt	43.3	41.9	40.6	39.5	38.3	40.7

Note: Windfall tax and associated spending included. Public net borrowing roughly equals Maastricht deficit. Net public debt is about 8% below gross.

Source: Economic and Fiscal Strategy Report, table 4.5

Cyclical differences in the past

In its Brown Paper the Treasury quotes recent evidence to show that in cyclical terms 'the UK became increasingly out of step with Germany during the 1980s, while the US and UK cycles have been relatively synchronised'. It also concedes that 'growth has been less volatile in [France and Germany] than in the UK.' As the Chancellor points out 'divergence is also a legacy of Britain's past susceptibility to boom and bust'. This state of affairs, far from being a reason why the British and continental cycles cannot converge, is a reason for seeking a more stable growth pattern by joining full EMU.

If EMU will in fact bring the UK lower interest rates than otherwise, this is a reason for joining as soon as possible, rather than an obstacle, except in the short-term. Lower and more stable interest rates, short-term and long-term, 'would create better conditions for businesses to make long-term decisions to invest in Britain', to quote the Chancellor's third of his five tests for EMU entry. This in its turn would raise the UK's rate of economic growth above what it would have been outside EMU.

The Chancellor's tests are so loosely defined that anyone will be able to say that they have been either passed or failed, according to the dictates of political expediency. A better test would be to compare life inside EMU with life outside. Britain will lose all claim to be 'at the heart of Europe' if the euro goes ahead without it. This in itself might not matter if there were decisive economic advantages in staying outside. The opposite is the case.

DISADVANTAGES OF STAYING OUT

Unstable exchange rate

Outside EMU, the Bank of England would continue to set UK short-term interest rates, with a limited degree of freedom in relation to foreign rates. In view of the exchange rate risk attaching to sterling, the Bank would probably have to set rates higher than euro rates to achieve a stable pound-euro exchange rate. Financial markets might nevertheless drive the pound up and down irrespective of relative interest rates, in response to many other factors. The Bank would thus not be able to control monetary conditions, which are a combination of the interest rate and the exchange rate.

With sterling the major European currency outside EMU, speculative foreign exchange dealing between it and the euro would increase, and the rate of exchange could become more volatile. If EMU had an external exchange rate policy, it would focus on the US dollar, and sterling would float freely against both the dollar and the euro. British business would be faced with massive exchange rate risks in the European single market, all the more so if its purchases and sales were determined in euro, while wage and other domestic costs continued to be set in sterling. Business investment and economic growth would suffer.

With the Bank of England responsible for a relatively tight monetary policy outside EMU, there would be pressure on the Treasury to relax fiscal policy to compensate. The Maastricht 3% deficit limit would no longer have any force were the UK to renounce its efforts to join EMU. Governments would increase budget deficits to stimulate economic activity, raising long-term interest rates, crowding out private sector borrowers, and increasing the risk of inflationary financing.

EMU better than stop-go

The independent UK model of economic management enjoyed a brief period in fashion in about 1994-97, when Britain temporarily grew faster than its continental partners. Now another phase of stop-go is in prospect, as the boom has turned out to be unsustainable, and wages are rising faster than in most industrial countries. The present slowdown will be a blessing in disguise, if it demonstrates conclusively to the British government and people that the stability afforded by a 15 member Euroland is preferable to the uncertainties of a medium-sized offshore country going it alone.

Once it is clear that the euro is going ahead successfully in 1999, the balance of argument will shift even further towards early British entry. Monetary union will advantage all its eleven members. The advantage to the UK of joining the Eleven once EMU is established will be even clearer than at present, but the advantage to the Eleven of admitting the UK will be correspondingly smaller, because the increase in the size of the monetary union will be relatively limited. The UK could thus be in trouble if other countries use its lack of exchange rate stability as a reason for making it wait on the touchline.

The long-term disadvantage of staying out is that the UK will be only a semi-detached member of the single market, and will be excluded from the new euro Council of finance ministers and the Governing Council of the European Central Bank. The UK will lose whatever influence it still has on the policies of the European Union. The UK will be a country of higher interest rates and less competitive, more protected banks and companies. Living standards will continue to fall down the European league table. Britain will pay a high price for the illusion of national political and economic independence.

8. EMU and the Press

Peter Riddell

During the 1975 referendum, Tony Benn argued that the overwhelming support of the national press for Britain remaining in the European Community was because newspaper proprietors 'reflect the economic interests which find the Common Market attractive'. On his view, proprietors inevitably look at the subject through capitalist spectacles. Nearly a quarter of a century on, Mr Benn's views on Europe have hardly changed. But the outlook of the 'capitalist' newspapers is very different. A majority of daily papers, particularly when measured by their relative sales, are now in the sceptic camp. This marked shift has become one of the main constraints on the Blair government's decisions over monetary union. Senior ministers cite the strong opposition of Rupert Murdoch's four News International titles, the Daily Mail group and Conrad Black's Telegraph papers as a serious obstacle to British participation. But why has this change in newspaper attitudes occurred and does it matter as much as both the media and Mr Blair's advisers believe?

In 1975, all the national papers, apart from the Morning Star, backed a yes vote on the question of whether Britain should remain in the European Community. Colin Seymour-Ure has argued that the press had a crucial role in determining the issues that dominated the referendum 'in the absence of a single, permanent, organised leadership and official orthodoxy on each side'.[1] Overall, 'the pro-Marketeers could hardly go wrong in their campaign faced with a sympathetic press and possessing nearly all the familiar faces'. Professor Seymour-Ure has calculated the treatment of each side 'as far as sympathetic column inches were concerned. Omitting the extreme case of the Morning Star, the mean balance was 54% pro and 21% anti (with the rest neutral content)'. But even those papers supporting a yes vote published opinion columns by leading opponents of British membership and devoted a considerable amount of space to the views of the antis. In some cases, such coverage may not have been helpful to the no cause since it focused on divisions in the Labour cabinet and the demonisation of its most vocal campaigner,

Mr Benn, as well as some unpleasant intrusions into his private life. Indeed, much of the coverage during the campaign dealt less with the campaign than with the implication of the internal Labour arguments for the future of the Wilson government with its tiny Commons majority. However, the preponderance of editorial coverage on the yes side was to some extent offset by heavy advertising by the no campaign. For instance, 'anti-Market advertising in the Daily Express occupied more than twice the space of anti-Market news'.

However, several of the papers who were most prominent in urging a yes vote in 1975 are now strongly sceptic in their opinions, notably The Times and the Daily Telegraph among the broadsheets and The Sun and the Daily Mail among the tabloids. It is hard to envisage The Sun repeating its centre-spread leader on the day of the referendum in 1975 when it took the line of 'Yes for a future together, No for a future alone'. In many papers, the tone of both news reports and leaders has often been highly critical of the European Union and the activities of the Commission and the Parliament. Nonetheless, the balance is not as sceptic as many pros often believe, and fear. Papers which already support British entry in their editorial or leader columns, in some cases earlier than the cautious Blair government's timetable, include the Mirror, the Independent and the Financial Times (though under half the latter's circulation of around 360,000 a day is now inside Britain). In addition, The Express will probably also support entry, not least because of the leading role that Lord Hollick, the paper's chairman, is playing in the campaign to argue for entry. The Guardian and the Observer have been critical of the government from the left, worried that the exchange rate is too high and monetary policy too restrictive, and they are unsympathetic to transferring control over interest rates to an unelected European Central Bank. But neither are exactly hardline sceptic papers. The government is anyway unlikely to call a referendum on monetary union until it is assured of a reasonable level of press support. The decision of Tony Blair and Gordon Brown to play the issue long, until after the next British general election, is partly based on the calculation that persuading these, and possibly other, newspapers will take time.

However, taking into account just daily national newspapers, and ignoring Sundays, support for entry from the Mirror (including the Daily Record in Scotland), the Express, the FT and the Independent would amount to a daily circulation of 4.5 m in favour of entry. On the other side can be counted The Sun, the Daily Mail, The Times and the Daily Telegraph with daily sales of 7.8 m. This leaves to one side the Daily

Star and The Guardian with combined average sales of 974,000. So there is clearly a substantial imbalance on the anti-EMU side, though a smaller one than many supporters of entry often believe. Nevertheless, this represents a clear reversal of the overwhelming balance the other way in 1975. Moreover, this shift is reinforced by differences in degrees of enthusiasm and commitment. In general, the opponents of British entry feel, and express themselves, more passionately than the supporters. For the former, joining a single currency — summed up in the tendentious phrase 'abolishing the pound' — is a threat almost to the very existence of Britain, while to many of the supporters of entry, the question is more one of balance, hedged round with all kinds of conditions and qualifications. It is wrong to exaggerate the importance of the stand taken in editorial columns which can be offset by reports in news pages and by the views of columnists. I have personally been completely free to express my generally supportive views towards the European Union and the single currency in the pages of The Times even though the paper's editorial line is strongly sceptic. However, such broad church pluralism is probably now the exception and, indeed, on several tabloids, like The Sun and the Daily Mail, a strongly sceptic line is seen not just in opinion pages but also throughout the news coverage where reporters are encouraged to present an anti-EU spin in their stories. The same is also true of the Telegraph papers.

Euro-sceptic proprietors

Many in the pro-European camp have attributed this shift in the balance of press attitudes to the takeover of certain titles by non-British companies and proprietors, the Australian turned American Rupert Murdoch and the Canadian Conrad Black. The argument runs that these two owners have little understanding of, and sympathy with, Britain's European interests, as opposed to its transatlantic ones, while their own companies have few investments in the rest of the European Union. There is something in this case, just as the division of opinion within business more generally is, in part, between multinationals with cross-European interests, like Unilever, and groups without such European holdings, like Hanson, or smaller businesses which still largely operate within the United Kingdom.

It is still also an ideological question. Messrs Murdoch and Black are both unapologetic advocates of the free market, deregulated model of Anglo-American capitalism: Mr Murdoch in a more adventurous, entrepreneurial way with a global sweep, and Mr Black in a more ponderous and limited fashion. They both dislike trade unions and excessive government regulation. For them, Brussels is a threat, not an opportunity. They are worried by regulation from Brussels and by everything implied by the term 'social Europe'. They have both benefited from, and were typical of, the Thatcher-Reagan era. Mr Black has become a public champion of an American rather than a European option. In a lecture to the Centre for Policy Studies in July 1998, Mr Black argued for a re-negotiation of Britain's membership of the European union to achieve 'a status not greatly different to Norway's: free movement of goods and people while avoiding political and judicial integration'.[2] While retaining the benefits of a European common market, he argued that Britain should join the North American Free Trade Agreement.

This scenario has become the latest fantasy of the sceptics, an alternative to Britain's current European position which, it is claimed, will preserve the benefits of open and free trade while incurring none of the obligations and costs. Not only is there no evidence that such a comfortable world is attainable, or negotiable, on the European side, but the chances of the American Congress approving such an arrangement for Britain are virtually non-existent. Mr Black cites the support for the idea of Newt Gingrich, the Speaker of the House of Representatives, as well as the Canadian leader of the Opposition. But Mr Gingrich's Atlanticist romanticism has little relation with the hard realities of Congressional attitudes on trade policy. However, this 'option' is being widely discussed among sceptics and is advocated in the sceptic press. But Mr Murdoch has always been more of a realist, concentrating on the financial interests of his global News Corporation group and willing to work with regimes of all kinds. What matters for him is what will help the growth of News Corporation, not the political colour of the governments with which he deals. A personal ideological preference for the Anglo-American over the European social model is only part of the story for Mr Murdoch, as was shown in The Sun's decision to back Tony Blair at the start of the 1997 election campaign.

Thatcherite journalists

As important as the views of the proprietors have been those of a younger generation of journalists which first came to public notice in the second half of the 1980s and achieved positions of influence, and power, in the early 1990s. These include Charles Moore, editor of the Daily Telegraph and formerly of The Spectator; Boris Johnson, a Conservative candidate in the 1997 election, a columnist on the Daily Telegraph and formerly that paper's boisterous Brussels correspondent; Simon Heffer, a historian and trenchant columnist on the Daily Mail, formerly with the Telegraph group; Paul Dacre, the populist and highly sceptic editor of the Daily Mail and successor in 1998 to the late Sir David English as that group's editor-in-chief; Peter Stothard, editor of The Times from 1992; Martin Ivens, whose influence has been more as a senior executive commissioning articles than as a writer, on both The Times and Sunday Times; and Matthew d'Ancona, who moved from The Times to the Sunday Telegraph, becoming its deputy editor and the intellectual voice of the younger right. These are all in some ways products of the Thatcher era and were influenced by her nationalist and increasingly hostile view of developments in Brussels, epitomised by her Bruges speech of September 1988.

These journalists were shaped less by the arguments of the Cold War era which convinced many of their predecessors about the desirability of closer European integration than by apparent triumph of the Anglo-American economic and security approach during the 1980s. They saw closer integration as a threat to the competitive position of Britain and doubted Europe's ability to work closely together on defence and foreign policy issues compared with Britain's traditional easy and close relations with the United States. This younger generation also became allied with a veteran group of right-wing columnists who had moved with Lady Thatcher to become more sceptical about Europe, such as Paul Johnson and William Rees-Mogg. After Lady Thatcher's departure in November 1990, these journalists all looked back to her era and compared it favourably with what followed, particularly following Black Wednesday in September 1992 when sterling was forced out of the exchange rate mechanism.

Anthony Seldon has written in his biography of John Major about the latter's largely unsuccessful attempts to court these journalists, most of whom viewed him with contempt.[3] He was seen by them as weak, both in his general handling of the government and more particularly over Europe. This attitude was shown most clearly during the Tory leadership contest of June/July 1995 when these writers, and their papers, were very hostile to Mr Major's re-election, hoping for an alternative leader who could not only revive the Tories' re-election prospects but also offer a more distinctive, and sceptic, line on Europe. Seldon concluded that: 'the loss of great swathes of the press, after all the efforts expended since 1995 to win them over, was both harbinger and part cause for the eventual scale of the defeat'.

Therefore, from the late 1980s onwards, committed sceptic journalists made the running on many of these papers, with the support and often active encouragement of their proprietors. But the emergence of this sceptic group of journalists was as important as the identity of the proprietors. In general, much of the press both reflected and stimulated an increasingly sceptic tone in the political debate over Europe. As the Tory party became more and more divided over Europe during the Major years, few leading Conservative politicians highlighted the advantages of Britain's membership of the EU, let alone the merits of a single currency. And while taking a more pro-European stand, the Labour opposition's main concern was to highlight divisions in the government. So the press was not alone in being largely defensive, rather than positive, on the European issue.

DOES EURO-SCEPTICISM MATTER?

If the sceptic shift in much, thought not all, the national press is clear, does it matter? The politicians clearly believe it does. Ahead of the 1997 general election, both the Major and Blair teams spent a lot of time trying to win back, or win, the support of the press. And both proprietors and editors liked being courted, seldom understating their own influence. Tony Blair and his advisers, notably Alastair Campbell, his chief press secretary and a successful former tabloid journalist, went to considerable lengths in the 1994-97 period to court The Sun in the hope of winning its support. This was not just because of the size of its readership but also because a high proportion of them were uncommitted swing voters. This wooing culminated in an article under Mr Blair's name on Monday 17 March 1997, the day that the election was formally called, when he made distinctly sceptic gestures while not betraying the substance of his pro-European policy. Describing himself as a 'British patriot', Mr Blair promised that he would 'not sell my country short' and 'we will have no truck with a European superstate. We will fight for Britain's interests and to keep our independence every inch of the way'. His tone allowed The Sun to proclaim that 'Blair takes hard new line on EU' with a leader claiming that his views bordered on the Euro-sceptic. That was storing up trouble for the future, as was seen in June 1998, but the immediate pay-off was The Sun's support for Mr Blair the following day.

The academic and survey evidence is that the impact of the press is less than either politicians fear or journalists claim. Over time, newspapers can influence the public debate, reinforcing and exaggerating trends, but not creating them. For instance, The Sun could never have convinced its readers in the 1997 election that Tony Blair was the type of incompetent and dangerous bungler that it portrayed Neil Kinnock as in the 1992 campaign. Martin Linton, the former Guardian journalist and now Labour MP, spent a lot of time during a research fellowship at Nuffield College seeking to prove that Kelvin MacKenzie was right to claim after the 1992 election that 'It's the Sun Wot Won It'.[4] He claims that the polls show that, while a majority of readers of The Sun were Labour voters for most of the 1987-92 period, they swung heavily to the Tories in the run-up to the election, when the paper's anti-Labour propaganda was at its most intense. In particular, in the three months before the election, the swing to the Conservatives was 8% among readers of The Sun, but zero among readers of the Mirror. It can alternatively be argued that this says more about the difference between the committed Labour supporters who read the Mirror and the less politically committed readers of The Sun than it necessarily does about the influence of the two papers. Mr Linton, however, argues that the character of the readers of The Sun has put 'a powerful weapon in the hands of certain press proprietors. It is too much to hope that they will not use it'.

The contrary view has been put by John Curtice, an academic and specialist in opinion research. He has argued, on the basis of panel studies which allow a longer-term insight into newspaper reading habits and voting intentions, that 'there is no evidence that those reading a Conservative inclined newspaper swung to the Conservatives more strongly than other voters during the course of the campaign itself'.[5] Although 'British newspapers do have some influence on the voting behaviour of individual readers, this influence is not powerful enough to have a substantial impact on the overall outcome'. Further research into trends in Tory support during John Major's worst troubles over Europe in 1992-95 shows that the decline was no greater among readers of papers that had become highly critical of the government than among readers of papers than remained generally loyal. Curtice concludes that, 'a strongly partisan press, particularly one that favours one party far more than the rest, may not be desirable. But whether it has much influence is another matter'.

The main reason to explain the limited direct impact of the press is that most of the public gets its political information from the broadcast media not newspapers. This is even though Britain has a much higher relative readership of papers than the rest of Europe. Broadcasters are under obligations of various kinds to provide balance in their coverage so the public has an alternative, non-partisan source of information, which it largely trusts, to the more partisan coverage of newspapers, which it often mistrusts. Nonetheless, the sceptic shift in the press during the 1990s has probably had a cumulative impact in influencing public attitudes, particularly in the absence of a clear lead from the politicians. In this respect, the problem lies more with the politicians than the media. It is the vacuum created by the politicians than has given the sceptics their chance.

Government calculations

On this view, the media, and particularly national newspapers, are not a fixed, or decisive, factor in the government's calculations over a single currency. They are only part of the equation. Indeed, the press responds to the public mood, as much as creating it. The government believes that public and press opinion can be won round. This is partly to do with fulfilling Gordon Brown's five conditions set out in October 1997, however nebulous most look in practice. But as important is the creation of a sense of inevitability about joining if EMU is successfully launched after January 1999. This will be partly about how EMU fares in the eleven participating countries but it also reflects the increasing use and familiarity with the euro in Britain itself. So the government hopes that by 2001-02, or whenever the next election is held, a majority of the public will accept entry as both desirable and obvious.

The Blair camp does not expect to win over all the sceptic press. Indeed, many sceptic politicians and journalists are already arguing that, however successful the first two or three years of the euro turn out to be, 2001 or 2002 is far too early for Britain to make a proper judgment on the merits of joining. So no one expects the Telegraph papers to come out for entry. Paul Dacre, editor-in-chief of the Mail group, is also a gut sceptic, much more so than his proprietor, Lord Rothermere, who backed a 'wait-and-see' approach: 'if it works, we all know we've got to join'. In an interview in August 1998, Lord Rothermere was quite relaxed about the contrast in views with the deeply sceptic Dacre: 'quite right too and so are most of our readers. Don't forget, the duty of a newspaper is to articulate the opinions of its readers'. But the Blair camp has not given up hope of persuading some of the News International papers.

Peter Mandelson, the Blair cabinet's shrewdest strategist, has publicly expressed the hope that Mr Murdoch can be converted to support for a single currency. During a television interview broadcast in April 1998, he said: 'at the end of the day, Rupert Murdoch would say ... if it's really in the interests of the British economy that we're in rather than out, if monetary union, the whole project, has been established, it's got under way, everyone's flocking to it and we are losing out economically and financially by being apart from it, I think that as a pragmatist he would say okay, we've got to go in'. These remarks also underline the importance that the Blair circle attaches to maintaining good relations with, and the support of, Mr Murdoch.

Implicit in the Mandelson view is that Mr Murdoch will ultimately be swayed by pragmatic, commercial factors and that any global media group has to have extensive interests on the continent of Europe. Mr Murdoch has discussed plenty of deals on the continent, in Germany, Spain and Italy, but he has found the going tough and has achieved the prominent position in the rest of Europe that his companies have in other markets. One factor may have been dislike of the stridently sceptic, and occasionally almost xenophobic, attitude of The Sun over the years, as well as hostility, especially in France, to someone epitomising Anglo-American capitalism at its most buccaneering. The implication is that if News Corporation wants to make a bigger impact in these still heavily regulated markets, then it will need to be less sceptic and warmer towards the European Union. Mr Murdoch will need friends if he is to complete the deals and achieves the market share that he wants. Hence, the argument runs, if the euro is a success, Mr Murdoch will warm to it. Mr Blair is therefore trying to draw Mr Murdoch more into Europe, as was shown by the row in March 1998 over a phone conversation between the British and Italian Prime Ministers about Mr Murdoch's chances of buying into Mediaset, Silvio Berlusconi's television company.

Perhaps. An alternative view is that, whatever happens between Mr Blair and Mr Murdoch, the love affair between New Labour and The Sun is bound to fall apart over Europe. The Sun is a populist, nationalist paper at heart and, as such, its support of the Blair government has always rested on a false premise. Mr Blair is not really a sceptic. He may be cautious in his tactics over entry into monetary union (too cautious for some of us) but he privately believes that Britain will join if the euro is successful. So his 'wait and see' posture is a tactical facade. On this view, there is bound to be a falling-out at some stage. That was shown in June 1998 following the Cardiff European Council when Mr Blair appeared to be taking a much friendlier stance towards the euro, partly to test the water. There was little immediate reaction from the sceptic press. The Financial Times then quoted a 'government member' as saying 'we ran up the euro flag and it has not been shot down. So we will probably keep it up there'. This produced an angry response from The Sun and its new editor David Yelland: a picture of a masked Tony Blair on its front page was accompanied by the headline 'Is this the most dangerous man in Britain?' There was more than a hint of the disillusioned lover, issuing a dramatic warning about being taken for granted in any gradual move towards membership of the single currency. But behind the headline lay the views of Trevor Kavanagh, The Sun's political editor, and Irwin Stelzer, who is a leading figure at the American Enterprise Institute but is, more significantly, one of Mr Murdoch's key advisers on economic and political issues.

Mr Kavanagh did not agree with The Sun's support for New Labour in the 1997 election, while both he and Mr Stelzer are passionate opponents of British membership of the euro. Mr Stelzer has argued that Mr Blair is being bounced into support by Gordon Brown, his Chancellor.[6] 'Worst of all, the Prime Minister's uncertainty about abandoning the pound in favour of the euro proved no match for the Iron Chancellor's certainty that it is in Britain's interests, as he sees them, to adopt the euro'. Like most Blair versus Brown stories, this rests on a mistaken assumption. The Prime Minister and Chancellor agree on the gradualist strategy of preparing Britain and public opinion for entry to the euro, even though their language sometimes differs.

Facing The Sun

At the end of the day, or rather in 2001-02, I expect the Blair government publicly to favour entry, so I doubt if The Sun can be won over from its instinctive and deeply felt opposition. Some of Mr Blair's advisers recognise this. Their hope is that, by promising to hold a referendum on joining a single currency after the next election, rather than before, they can isolate the issue. The implicit promise to The Sun is 'judge us on our whole record at the general election, and then you can fight us on the euro at a later referendum'. This is fanciful. If the euro has been launched successfully, the question of whether Britain joins is bound to be the central issue of the general election, particularly with William Hague believing that 'saving the pound' will be a powerful rallying cry against the government. So Mr Blair and Mr Brown will have to declare their hand by the time of the election, if not before.

The Blair government is therefore likely to have to take a decision with a significant proportion of the press hostile to entry. This is in itself unlikely to be decisive if other circumstances are favourable, not just the euro's successful launch but also, in particular, whether the government has taken a lead in the previous few years. There is evidence, as Peter

Kellner discusses, that opinion can be moved provided such a clear lead is given by the politicians. That happened in the run-up to the 1975 referendum. And since the 1997 general election, the generally more positive, if hardly enthusiastic, tone of the Blair government's comments about Europe have been matched by a reduction in hostility towards the EU in the polls.

MORI has been undertaking a regular series of polls on public attitudes to British entry into monetary union for Salomon Smith Barney. These show a clear reduction in the balance against membership, from minus 27% (those in favour less those against) at the time of the general election to minus 17% in July 1998. This last poll was taken after The Sun's spectacular blast against Tony Blair raised the profile of the European issue. Nonetheless, the biggest shift in opinion occurred among readers of tabloids, and Labour and Liberal Democrat supporters, than among readers of the broadsheets. Tabloid readers remain, however, strongly against British entry. Readers of The Sun are still by a long way the most hostile. But readers of the Mirror, Daily Mail and Daily Express have become markedly less hostile to a single currency during the course of 1998. MORI also puts the question in a slightly different form by asking about attitudes 'if the government were strongly to urge that Britain should be part of a single European currency'. This kind of question gave a better guide to the actual outcome of the 1975 referendum than the more familiar 'how would you vote?' question. On this basis, the negative balance in July 1998 was minus 7% with readers of the broadsheets in favour by a 10% margin, and readers of the tabloids against by 16%. This is a much smaller gap than existed before the 1975 campaign started.

The Blair government can probably win a referendum on entry in three or four years' time, depending on what happens to the euro and the state of the British economy. The more hostile attitude of parts of the press compared with 1975 is a complicating factor but not necessarily an insurmountable problem, unless the politicians allow it to be so. All depends on how quickly, and how clearly, the government gives a lead.

[1] Colin Seymour-Ure, 'Press' in David Butler and Uwe Kitzinger, The 1975 Referendum, London, Macmillan, 1976.

[2] Conrad Black, 'Britain's Final Choice: Europe or America?', Centre for Policy Studies, 1998.

[3] Anthony Seldon, *Major, A Political Life*, London, Weidenfeld and Nicolson, 1997, pp. 707-13.

[4] Martin Linton, 'Maybe The Sun won it after all', in British Journalism Review, vol. 7, no. 2, 1996.

[5] John Curtice, 'Is the Sun Shining on Tony Blair? The Electoral Influence of British Newspapers', in The Harvard International Journal of Press/Politics, Spring 1997, vol. 2, no. 2.

[6] Irwin Stelzer, 'Brown Bosses Blair', The Spectator, 27 June 1998.

9. EMU and Public Opinion

Peter Kellner

At first glance, one of Labour's rashest promises at the 1997 general election was to hold a referendum on British membership of the single currency should the government deem that entry is desirable. Almost every survey that has been conducted so far shows a significant majority for keeping the pound. Hostility to the euro is not as great as it was before Tony Blair became prime minister: a three-to-one rejection of the single currency in November 1996 had shifted to a margin of less than two-to-one a year later. But the 'noes' still have it.

TABLE ONE

Q. If there were a referendum now on whether Britain should be part of a single European currency, how would you vote?

	In favour	Against	Don't know
November 1991	33%	54%	13%
November 1994	33	56	11
June 1995	29	60	11
May 1996	23	60	17
November 1996	22	64	14
April 1997	27	54	19
October 1997	27	54	19
November 1997	30	52	18
January 1998	32	52	16
March 1998	30	54	15
May 1998	31	54	15
July 1998	33	50	17

Q. If the government were to strongly urge that Britain should be a part of a single European currency, how would you vote?

	In favour	Against	Don't know
November 1997	38%	47%	15%
January 1998	38	47	14
March 1998	36	51	13
May 1998	36	50	14
July 1998	39	46	16

Source: MORI for Salomon Smith Barney

Could the tide now be turning? A European Commission survey, which was not intended for publication but which was leaked to The Guardian (30 July 1998), produced a startling result. It found that in June 1998, as many as 46% agreed that 'there should be a single currency, the euro, replacing the pound and all the other EU currencies' — up from a previous maximum of 42% — while 49% disagreed, down from 53% the previous month (Table Two). These figures should be treated with some caution, for the survey, conducted by Euroquest MRB, consisted of a sample of just 800 adults. The margin of error is 4%; on its own, the survey might signal nothing more than a rogue poll.

The good news for the pro-euro camp is that MORI's late-July poll for stockbrokers Salomon Smith Barney, among a sample of more than 2000, also showed a narrowing of the gap; the bad news is that it failed to confirm the near-level-pegging figures of the Euroquest survey.

On its main question, MORI found that 'if there were a referendum now', 50% would vote to keep the pound, while 33% would vote to replace it with the euro. This 17 point gap is the narrowest that MORI has recorded in the seven years that it has been testing the issue. When MORI asked the same people how they would vote 'if the Government were to urge strongly that Britain should be part of a single European currency', the gap is reduced to just seven points, again, narrower than before.

Q. Do you agree or disagree that 'There should be a single currency, the euro, replacing the pound and all the other EU currencies'?

	Agree	Disagree	Don't Know
January 1996	34%	62%	4%
February 1996	30	66	4
April 1996	34	61	5
May 1996	31	64	5
June 1996	29	67	4
July 1996	34	61	5
September 1996	33	63	4
October 1996	35	60	5
November 1996	28	65	7
December 1996	33	63	4
January 1997	32	64	4
February 1997	32	63	5
March 1997	31	64	5
April 1997	29	66	5
May 1997	29	66	5
June 1997	27	67	6
July 1997	28	67	5
September 1997	30	65	5
October 1997	28	62	10
November 1997	39	53	8
January 1998	36	59	5
February 1998	31	62	7
March 1998	42	55	3
April 1998	42	52	6
May 1998	40	53	7
June 1998	46	49	5

Source: Euroquest MRB for the European Commission

So do the latest MORI and Euroquest results depict a short-lived blip or a more lasting trend? It is too early to say. All we can be sure of is that the anti-euro lobby is larger than the pro-euro camp, and, the Euroquest survey notwithstanding, probably by a significant margin. Unless and until a series of polls show a sustained change in public attitudes, the best assessment is that the 'no' vote outnumbers the 'yes' vote by about 20 points, with the precise margin fluctuating either side of that number month by month.

Politically, the task still looks daunting for those who would seek to abolish the pound. So has the prime minister made a huge strategic mistake in his policy towards the euro, and in particular his promise to hold a referendum? Is he likely to be humiliated by a public rejection of a central feature of his strategy for taking Britain into the next millennium — a new, closer and more constructive relationship with the rest of the European Union? Or might the public hostility during most of the Nineties convert into popular support for the euro over the next three or four years?

As polling organisations never tire of repeating, surveys measure public attitudes at a moment in time. They do not predict the future. Even so, by looking behind the headline figures, and by delving into the past record of public attitudes to Europe, it is possible to assess the forces at work, and to make a plausible estimate of how opinion might evolve in the run-up to a referendum.

The first, and most important, point to make about British opinion is that only a minority hold fixed views, either for or against the euro. Two different organisations, asking differently-worded questions at different times, discovered a remarkably similar range of attitudes, with around three electors out of five supporting a 'wait and see' stance (see Table Three).

The minority rejecting the single currency outright is larger than the minority of euro-enthusiasts; however, both groups are far smaller than the majority who do not wish to commit themselves firmly one way or the other. This indicates that opinion is potentially fluid. If the conditions are right, opposition to the euro may melt away.

Q. If other countries create a single European currency, what should Britain do?

Decide to join straightaway   14%

Leave the decision open with the possibility of joining later   60%

Decide never to join   20%

Don't know   6%

Source: Opinion Research Business for the European Commission, February 1997

Q. Which of the following statements about British membership of the European single currency most closely represents your view:

Membership will offer advantages, and Britain should join as soon
as possible   14%

Membership could offer advantages, but Britain should only join
when the economic conditions are right   57%

Britain should rule out the possibility of membership for at least
10 years   20%

Don't know / no opinion   8%

Source:MORI for the European Movement, January 1998

What are the conditions that could produce a 'yes' majority in a referendum? In 1996, and again in its survey for the European Movement in January 1998, MORI explored the significance of economic factors. On both occasions it found that around half the public acknowledged that they would be swayed by judgements about the impact of the single currency on Britain's economy. The number of out-and-out opponents of the euro fell between the two surveys, and the number of enthusiasts increased; but, once again, the size of these two minorities on both occasions was significantly less than the number who admitted that economic prospects would sway their judgements.

As with all polls that seek to measure possible public reactions to hypothetical future events, one must take care with the precise figures. Voters are often bad predictors of their own future behaviour. However, experience suggests that many people err, if anything, on the side of predicting consistency in their attitudes. If half of all electors say that economic judgements may cause them to rethink their views on the euro, the true figure is more likely to be higher, rather than lower.

TABLE FOUR

Q. As you may know, the member states of the European Union are making plans for a European single currency to start in 1999. Which of the following best describes your own view of British participation in the single currency?

	August 1996	*January 1998*
I strongly support British participation	10%	17%
I am generally in favour of British participation, but could be persuaded against it if I thought it would be bad for the British economy	27%	27%
I am generally opposed to British participation, but could be persuaded in favour of it if I thought it would be good for the British economy	21%	24%
I strongly oppose British participation	33%	23%
Don't know / no opinion	9%	9%

Source: MORI for the European Movement

What is more, the evidence is that so far, the euro is seen as an economic threat more than an economic opportunity. A MORI poll for *The Sun* in November 1997 found that only 24% thought interest rates would be 'very likely (7%) or 'fairly likely' (17%) to fall if Britain joined the single currency; as many as 59% regarded lower interest rates as 'very unlikely' (25%) or 'fairly unlikely' (34%). On unemployment, expectations were more evenly divided on whether the numbers would rise or fall. What is clear, however, is that only a minority — and in the case of interest rates, only a quarter of the public — believe that the euro would bring economic blessings. It follows that if this belief changes, then so could support for the euro itself. If the euro's interest rate remains lower than Britain's from 1999 on, and if, therefore, British membership seems likely to result in cheaper mortgages, then one of the main reasons why so many people dislike the euro today will disappear.

Economics, however, will not be the only battleground. Sovereignty is also bound to be a major issue in any referendum campaign. And there is no doubt that most people are wary of giving extra powers to European institutions. Much of this wariness flows from a lack of trust in the European Union. The spring 1998 edition of the European Commission's *Eurobarometer*, reporting surveys conducted in October and November 1997, found that only 23% of Britons 'tend to trust' the EU, while 48% 'tend not to trust' the EU. Sweden is the only EU member state where fewer people trust the Union. If a referendum is to produce a 'yes' majority for joining the single currency, trust in Europe's institutions must rise.

However, the arguments about sovereignty do not simply revolve round trust of the EU. It is perfectly possible to have a high opinion of the competence and efficiency of the European Commission, say, yet still feel that sovereignty is too precious to give away. Last year's Opinion Research Business poll for the European Commission sought to test the trade-off between economic gain and sovereignty-loss. As Table Five shows, only one person in three says that they would put retention of sovereignty ahead of greater prosperity

TABLE FIVE

Q. If the single European currency goes ahead and Britain were to take part, would you be prepared to accept some loss of economic sovereignty if, in return, it leads to higher living standards?

Yes	53%
No	31%
Don't know	16%

Source: Opinion Research Business for European Commission, February 1997

These polls do not prove that the economic arguments are bound to sway voters towards the euro; they do, however, suggest strongly that the argument can be won. Most people currently hold only weak views on the subject. If enough people are persuaded that British membership of the euro will increase prosperity, then this may well overcome fears of loss of sovereignty. If the euro's interest rates start low and remain low, then millions of home-owners payers might face a choice: vote 'yes' for cheaper mortgages, or 'no' for rates to stay high. The prospect of saving, say, £1000 a year (the result of 2% reduction in the mortgage rate on a loan of £50,000) would be very tempting.

There is, however, a more fundamental issue that may sway public opinion. At present, the euro does not exist. To propose joining it is to ask people to take a leap in the dark. By the time a referendum is held, say in autumn 2001 or the spring of 2002, the euro will have existed for more than two years. The circulation of notes and coins will either be imminent or have already started. Instead of being a 'leap-in-the-dark' issue, a referendum on the single currency could become a 'risk-of-being-left-behind' issue. The potency of this shift is illustrated by a survey conducted by NOP for BBC's *Newsnight* and *The Independent* at the time of the Maastricht Treaty in 1991.

TABLE SIX

Q. Some countries in the European Community are considering plans to go beyond economic cooperation and create a political union. Do you agree or disagree with these statements on this issue:

a) **'The British government should do all it can to prevent the creation of a European political union'**

b) **'If the rest of the EC decides to create a political union, Britain can't afford to be left out'.**

	A. Prevent political union	B. Can't afford to be left out
Agree	40%	64%
Disagree	36%	18%
Neither / Don't know	24%	18%

Source: NOP for Independent/BBC Newsnight, November 1991

As Table 6 shows, 40% were hostile to political union, but this number fell to just 18% when respondents were confronted with the prospect that political union might happen and the risk of Britain being left behind. The proportion giving a pro-political union response jumped from 36 to 64%.

Older history also suggests that initial hostility to British involvement in Europe tends to reduce as the issue moves from the edge of the political stage towards the centre, and decisions become imminent. Gallup recorded public attitudes from the June 1970 general election, which was won by the Conservatives under Edward Heath, who had promised to reopen negotiations on British entry, until Britain joined the Common Market on 1 January 1973.

Table Seven shows that the mid-1970 to mid-1971 figures for supporting entry into the Common Market were even lower than the 1991-97 figures for joining the euro. But opinion shifted sharply after Parliament voted decisively in 1971 in favour of joining; and the pros and antis were evenly divided around January 1972, when Britain signed the Treaty of Accession.

TABLE SEVEN

Q. Do you approve or disapprove of the Government applying for membership of the Common Market?

	Approve	Disapprove	Don't know
June 1970	23%	57%	20%
August 1970	21	56	23
October 1970	22	56	22
December 1970	16	66	18
January 1971	22	58	20
May 1971	23	59	18
July 1971	24	60	16

Q. On the facts as you know them are you for or against Britain Joining the Common Market?

	For	Against	Don't know
August 1971	36%	47%	17%
October 1971	32	51	17
November 1971	44	41	15
December 1971	38	47	15
February 1972	42	41	17
April 1972	43	43	14
May 1972	41	45	14
July 1972	36	51	13
September 1972	40	42	15
October 1972	39	41	20
December 1972	38	45	16

Source: Gallup

The build-up to the 1975 referendum produced a similar transformation in public attitudes. During the October 1974 general election, when Labour moved from minority government to a tiny overall majority in the House of Commons, Harold Wilson promised to renegotiate the terms of Britain's membership of the Common Market, and put the results to a referendum.

As Table 8 shows, a clear majority at the time of the election favoured withdrawal. But when the same people were asked how they would vote in a referendum 'if the Government negotiated new terms for Britain's membership of the Common Market and they thought it was in Britain's interests to remain a member', then a two-to-one majority supported staying in — which proved to be very close to the result of the actual referendum eight months later. (As Table One shows, MORI's recent polls for Salomon Smith Barney have asked a similar 'what if' question, but found only a modest increase in support for the euro; but the modesty of the 'what if' effect may reflect the fact that a referendum is still some way over the political horizon. The effect may increase if and when the prospect is more imminent.)

As Gallup's main tracking question shows, there was a 20-point swing in favour of remaining a member of the Common Market between early February and mid March 1975, a period that culminated in the decision of the Wilson cabinet on 18 March to support the renegotiated terms.

TABLE EIGHT

Q. (a) If you could vote tomorrow on whether we should stay in the Common Market or leave it, how would you vote?

Q. (b) If the Government negotiated new terms for Britain's membership of the Common Market and they thought it was in Britain's interests to remain a member, how would you vote then?

[figures exclude don't knows]

	(a) Tomorrow to stay in	(a) Tomorrow to leave	(b) Renegotiate to stay in	(b) Renegotiate to leave
October 1974	39	61	69	31
November 1974	45	55	72	28
February 1975	45	55	71	29
Early March 1975	57	43	76	24
Mid March 1975	64	36		
Early April 1975	63	37		
Late April 1975	64	36		
Early May 1975	65	35		
Mid May 1975	64	36		
Late May 1975	67	33		
5 June 1975 - Referendum result	67	33		

Source: Gallup

The consistent lesson of history, then, is that the 'default' position of the British public is hostility to closer involvement in Europe, by margins of between two-to-one and three-to-one, when the issue is in the back of people's minds; but that attitudes change sharply when domestic politics forces it to the front — and especially when the government of the day, backed by senior members of the main opposition party (as in 1971-72, when Roy Jenkins led a substantial minority of Labour MPs in opposing their own front bench and backing Heath, and 1975, when a number of senior Tories campaigned for a 'yes' vote in that year's referendum), takes a strongly pro-European stand.

Clearly, there can be no guarantee that history will repeat itself. A referendum in 2001 or 2002 on joining the euro may be lost. But the message from the polls of the past three decades is that recent hostility to the single currency certainly can be, and probably will be, overcome, if the government mounts a sufficient strong and broadly-based campaign, and is able to demonstrate that significant economic benefits will flow from Britain's membership.

10. The Euro and Parliamentary Democracy

PART ONE: WESTMINSTER

Nigel Forman

Of all the charges which are laid against Economic and Monetary Union and the euro, those of unaccountability and illegitimacy are perhaps the most telling, at any rate for those who care about the political process as much as policy outcomes. It is not surprising, therefore, that even those who favour British participation in EMU and the replacement of sterling with the euro seek convincing reassurances that these steps can be taken without creating a larger democratic deficit in the EMU area. The purpose of this contribution is to analyse more closely this problem from the perspective of the UK parliament at Westminster.

Accountability and legitimacy

A literal definition of accountability would imply responsibility and comprehensibility. Legitimacy must be presumed to mean notions of legality and propriety. Yet dictionary definitions of these terms are a good deal less exacting than those given by the British political class. Most Westminster politicians of all parties would hold that accountability should include the right of the people's elected representatives to criticise, complain, amend and, if necessary, overturn the decisions of those responsible for executive action. In the case of legitimacy, the notions of legality and propriety are obviously necessary components of the democratic ideal; but British political culture has come to attach a stronger meaning to the term, including the idea that the actions of executive bodies should have at least the implied support of the people as registered by a vote in parliament.

It is likely, therefore, to be difficult to persuade the people of Britain who care about these democratic processes and safeguards that membership of EMU will be both accountable and legitimate. Even assuming direct public endorsement of the idea in a national referendum early in the new century, it is likely that there will be a significant minority of politicians, business people and others who will never accept it.

Since all the monetary decisions which really matter in EMU, with the exceptions of exchange rate policy and the management of public debt, are meant to be taken by the European Central Bank, it is necessary to be clear about the various degrees of accountability which may be attainable. At one end of the spectrum there is the possibility that the ECB will be effectively unaccountable, because its Executive Board and Governing Council will interpret the legal position of the ECB and the subordinate national central banks as one of complete and unfettered independence 'when exercising the powers and carrying out the tasks and duties conferred upon them by this Treaty and this Statute'.[1]

Then there is the strong probability that there will be a degree of accountability in the ECB's performance of its duties as defined in Article 2 of the Protocol, but this will constitute no more than what might be described as a soft version of accountability, that is, one in which the ECB's executive actions are reasonably open and transparent, although probably not to the extent that those of the Bank of England or the US Federal Reserve are now. Indeed, when Wim Duisenberg was answering questions from Members of the European Parliament during their scrutiny of his appointment as President of the Bank on 7 May 1998, he said: 'I think it is important for the European System of Central Banks to be open, transparent and accountable, while being independent'; a position from which he deduced that 'the ESCB should explain its policy decisions to all interested parties, including the European Parliament and the public at large'. It is also worth noting that in these confirmation hearings Mr Duisenberg said that he had 'considerable difficulties' with the French proposal that the National Assembly should be able to question and hold to account ECB officials on the ostensible ground that if this facility were available to one national parliament, it would have to be made available to all.[2]

Third, there is the more remote possibility that the dynamics of European integration after January 1999, and certainly beyond July 2002, will be such that a hard version of accountability will be demanded and eventually achieved by the people and their elected representatives. This would imply that the President, Vice-President and the four other members of the ECB Executive Board might become subject to criticism and, in dire circumstances, vulnerable to dismissal by the European

Parliament (but not the national Parliaments) for reasons of perceived policy failure, and not simply for 'serious misconduct' as defined in Article 11.4 of the Protocol. However, in view of the high degree of legalism already enshrined in the acquis communautaire over nearly five decades, and the Treaty requirement that only the European Court of Justice may finally adjudicate on matters of disciplinary or institutional dispute, it seems on the face of it unlikely that MEPs will ever be able to subject the ECB to anything like such requirements of public accountability. The hard version of accountability is therefore almost certain to remain a political pipe-dream.

Theory and practice in the United Kingdom

To get a clear perspective upon how accountability for monetary policy is likely to change in the event that the UK adopts the euro, it is necessary first to describe present theory and practice in the United Kingdom. This provides a benchmark for future developments.

In a Memorandum of 25 September 1997 on the parliamentary accountability of public bodies, the Cabinet Office described the Bank of England as an 'associated public body of HM Treasury', and confirmed that it fell fairly and squarely within the remit of the House of Commons Treasury Select Committee in terms of parliamentary control.[3] This dry terminology may have represented the orthodoxy of the time, but since then the Bank of England has achieved a degree of operational independence (as opposed to goal-setting independence) under the 1998 Bank of England Act. This was described by the Chancellor as a 'new openness and accountability in [monetary] decision making that involves the Treasury Committee and the House of Commons in a far bigger way than ever before'. It is certainly true that under the arrangements introduced by the Labour government there is potential for the executors of British monetary policy to be held to account in parliament to a greater extent than previously. British arrangements for parliamentary accountability of British monetary policy now stand well in comparison with other EU member states. Indeed, the OECD found that 'in international comparison, the United Kingdom's framework is among the strongest in terms of accountability and transparency'.[4]

As far as the Treasury Select Committee is concerned, there are many dimensions to what it can do on behalf of parliament as a whole, notwithstanding that 'accountability is an elusive concept and trying to find an accurate and comprehensive definition is correspondingly difficult'. The Committee can correspond directly with the Bank of

131

England on matters of monetary policy; it can take evidence from the Chancellor and the Governor on the inflation target; it can hold hearings at least twice a year on the Bank's Quarterly Inflation Report; it can assert its claim to hold confirmation hearings for those appointed or reappointed as Governor, Deputy Governor or members of the Monetary Policy Committee; it can take evidence as frequently or infrequently as it likes from the Governor and his senior colleagues at the Bank on their general stewardship of monetary policy; it can take evidence on the Bank's Annual Report to Parliament, including evidence from the non-executive members of the Court; it can question the Governor in the event that he has to write an open letter to the Chancellor stating the reasons why the rate of inflation has diverged by more than 1% from the government's target; and it can question both the Chancellor and the Governor in the unlikely event that the former has to use his statutory power to override the Bank in its operation of monetary policy.

By any measure, this is an impressive panoply of parliamentary power designed to hold to account not only those whose responsibility it is to define the objectives of British monetary policy but also those who are charged with the operational duties of carrying it out.[5] The net effect of these new arrangements was well summarised in the Select Committee Report:

'The Treasury Committee's responsibility in relation to monetary policy is to provide a forum for it to be examined by exposing to public scrutiny the thinking and actions of those responsible for its formulation and delivery. ... The Bank can thus be held accountable to the public as well as to Parliament through being more open and transparent and by having to explain its actions in an independent forum. It is in this respect that our Committee can most effectively and most appropriately exercise its role of holding the Bank accountable'.

Theory and practice in Euroland

We know that eleven of the fifteen member states of the European Union will participate in EMU from 1 January 1999 and that, barring accidents, the same number or possibly more will adopt the euro in place of their own national currencies for all transactions from 1 July 2002 at the latest. We also know what is written in the Protocol of the Maastricht Treaty which provides the legal basis for the ECB. In the 53 articles of the Protocol there is only one explicit reference, the appointments procedure aside, to anything resembling regular parliamentary accountability for

HOW THE COMMONS DEALS
WITH THE BANK OF ENGLAND

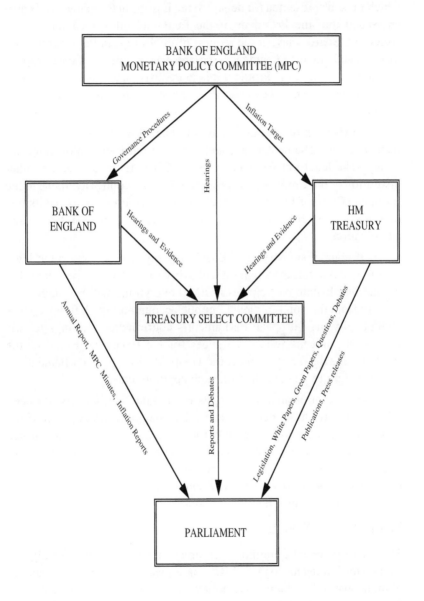

the actions of the Central Bank. Article 15, entitled *Reporting commitments*, obliges the Bank to publish quarterly reports on the activities of the ESCB, a weekly consolidated financial statement, and an annual report on the activities of the ESCB and its monetary policy, which must be presented for debate to the European Parliament. It is also envisaged that the President of the ECB and other members of the Executive Board 'may, at the request of the European Parliament or on their own initiative, be heard by the competent committees of the European Parliament', and in the Protocol it is graciously stated that these reports and statements 'shall be made available to interested parties free of charge'.[6]

Nowhere in the Treaty is any reference to be found to the role of member state parliamentary accountability for European Union monetary policy. The legal independence of the ECB is fettered, like any other institution of the Union, by the powers of judicial control available to the European Court of Justice under Article 35 of the Protocol in that its acts of omission or commission are open to review, interpretation and adjudication.

Of course, supporters of EMU may say that, whatever the legal position, in practice the situation will evolve after 1 January 1999 so that by the time Britain participates in EMU everything will be much more healthy from the point of view of public accountability. A first step was undoubtedly the European Parliament's confirmation hearings for Mr Duisenberg and his fellow nominees for the Executive Board of the ECB, despite the fact that, under the Treaty, the European Parliament has only the right to be consulted on such appointments.

Any claim of analogous rights by national parliaments has been rejected by Mr Duisenberg. It seems that the political evolution of the Union will have to have gone far before national MPs are able to enforce the soft version of accountability now available at Westminster. Closer concertation between the treasury committees of the member state parliaments could provide Mr Duisenberg and his colleagues with an acceptable forum for a regular dialogue.

What if the UK joins

The Treasury Select Committee has already recognised quite openly that 'should the UK decide to join EMU, ... new mechanisms for accountability of monetary and exchange rate policy would be required'.[7] This may be a significant understatement, because Britain's entry into EMU would render obsolete the current arrangements for parliamentary accountability.

This is for a number of obvious reasons, namely that the British government would have given up its power to set an inflation target for the UK, the Monetary Policy Committee of the Bank of England would have been reduced at best to a national advisory body and would probably need to be put out of its misery, and the Chancellor would have lost his right to override the Bank on monetary policy in exceptional circumstances.

It would be more accurate to say that once the UK is part of EMU and has the euro as its currency for all purposes, any version of merely national accountability for EU monetary policy is likely to be diluted and remote from the real centre of monetary decision making. Any participation by British MPs and their colleagues in the other national parliaments could only be indirect, and would be essentially by grace and favour of their counterparts in the European Parliament, who by that time are likely to have become fully-fledged rivals rather than partners in the battles for influence and power in the European Union.

According to the government, it is realistic to assume that the economy could be in a position to allow the UK to join EMU early in the next parliament, although serious doubts have recently been expressed about whether euro notes and coins could be produced in sufficient quantities for the UK's needs in less than three years following a clear public decision to participate. Yet nowhere in Mr Brown's response to the Treasury Select Committee Report on preparations for the third stage of EMU did he comment upon the parliamentary or public accountability of the project.[8] It is tempting to conclude that the policy of Tony Blair and Gordon Brown is one of tactical myopia when looking forward to this most significant aspect of our economic and monetary future.

While the Chancellor was keen to celebrate the 'new openness and accountability' of the Bank of England in his statement to the House of Commons in May 1997, and prepared to insist upon the 'provision and disclosure of information' in the Bank of England Act, it is important to realise that none of these commendable national procedures of accountability will operate with the same power and effect once the euro has become the sole legal currency.

The independence of the ECB and of the subordinate national central banks will be fully protected by Article 7 of its Protocol, although it can be expected to develop a rich dialogue with Ecofin and the European Parliament. Westminster and the other member state parliaments will be left with powers of democratic scrutiny over their own national central bank governors, all members of the Governing Council of the ESCB; they will also be left with democratic control over their own ministerial representatives on Ecofin and, through both processes, will exercise some indirect influence upon European monetary policy. But the influence of any one member state or any single national parliament will be attenuated, because 'general orientations for exchange rate policy', in the words of Article 109(2) (**Article 111(2)**), will be determined by a qualified majority in the Council, and the independence of the ECB and of the subordinate national central banks will be fully protected by the Treaty.

Member state parliaments may cooperate via the conferences of their European affairs committees, possibly supplemented by the concerted actions of parliamentary offices in Brussels on the lines of those already established by Denmark and Finland. They may also try to piggy-back on the European Parliament by participating periodically in a 'European Economic Forum', although it seems likely that in any such power-sharing arrangements the European Parliament will be in the driving seat because of its superior locus standi under the Treaties.

In the end it is difficult to avoid a fairly hard-hitting threefold conclusion. First, there will be less accountability for EU monetary policy in EMU than there is now under the current national arrangements in the UK. Second, the position of Westminster and other national parliaments will be more marginal in terms of real influence over economic and monetary policy than it is now. Third, this uneven institutional balance between EU forces on the one hand and national parliamentarians on the other *could* turn out to be beneficial for the European public interest *if* both parties are committed to enhancing the popular legitimacy of the euro. The cumulative decisions of the ECB could prove to be both right and popular over a long period of time — something which has been achieved in Germany with the Bundesbank, but which in the wider European context will require considerable suspension of disbelief.

[1] Article 7 of the Protocol on the Statute of the European System of Central Banks and the European Central Bank.

[2] Agence Europe, 8 May 1998.

[3] First Report of the House of Commons Treasury Select Committee, Session 1997-98, on *Accountability of the Bank of England*, Appendix 5.

[4] OECD Economic Survey, *United Kingdom*, June 1998, p. 36.

[5] The House as a whole also has a role in enforcing parliamentary accountability which could find expression in annual debates on the Bank of England on the basis of its annual report and possibly in adjournment debates initiated by individual MPs.

[6] Article 109b(3) (**Article 113(3)**).

[7] Fifth Report of the House of Commons Treasury Select Committee, Session 1997-98 on *The UK and preparations for Stage Three of Economic and Monetary Union*, para. 15.

[8] See Sixth Special Report of the House of Commons Treasury Select Committee, Session 1997-98, letter from the Chancellor of the Exchequer to the Chairman of the Committee.

PART TWO: THE EUROPEAN PARLIAMENT

John Stevens

Central Banks are usually said to be accountable when their operations are subject, directly or indirectly, to the scrutiny and control of parliaments elected by universal suffrage. Public authorities in general are likewise said to be legitimate primarily if they enjoy the support, or at least the sufferance, of a majority of the people over whom their powers are exercised. There exists, in fact, a sort of natural synergy between accountability and legitimacy, which is the primacy of the democratic principle. On this basis, the new European Central Bank would seem to be neither accountable nor legitimate. It is widely recognised that the Maastricht Treaty grants it a greater degree of independence than that enjoyed by any other existing central bank. It is an untested institution, managing a currency, the introduction of which is viewed, by most ordinary citizens, with resignation rather than enthusiasm.

Can it be, then, that EMU, probably the most significant geopolitical development in the world today and certainly a most ambitious economic initiative, is fatally flawed by a lack of democracy? In the tortuous British debate on the single currency, this has become the principle issue. Opponents of entry, such as William Hague, have picked on the non democratic nature of the ECB to argue that, because democracy is only real at a national rather than European level, EMU must fail, since rage against the impact of a uniform monetary policy upon individual participating countries can find no outlet against 'unelected bankers in Frankfurt'. In his speech to INSEAD in May 1998 and in similar subsequent declarations, Mr Hague has painted an especially lurid picture of civil disorder and even warfare because of the 'basically illegitimate nature of the ECB'.

It is true that, under the Maastricht Treaty, the only significant political influence upon the ECB's policy is in the appointment of its President and Executive Board and of the national central bank governors on its Governing Council by the heads of government of the participating states, who are themselves obviously accountable to their respective national parliaments (or directly to the electorate in the case of the President of France). It could be argued that the messy compromise over

Wim Duisenberg's appointment introduced the possibility of such influence becoming on-going, rather than once only at their appointment. This is especially credible since the European Parliament, having declared in the most solemn manner, through a statement by its President, that it had no intention of endorsing any such split-term, compromise arrangement, promptly proceeded to do exactly that.

On the other hand, the whole episode, far from being praised as showing political control over 'unelected bankers' was widely condemned, even by those who, in other circumstances, complain most vociferously about the undemocratic nature of EMU. Certainly, for the governments concerned, the May 1998 summit was felt to be so abrasive an exercise that the chances in the future of split terms for the President and other Board or Council members, and similar shenanigans, has been substantially diminished if not wholly eradicated. If there was bound to be a bust up of this kind at some point, may be it was better to have it at the outset; and EMU probably got off lightly with Messrs Duisenberg and Trichet, both of whose reputations for operational independence are unimpeached.

The rococo circumstances surrounding his appointment ironically has also made it much easier for Mr Duisenberg to reject, out of hand, requests from the national parliaments of Euroland for regular formal meetings. He has made plain that the only parliament he will deal with is the European Parliament, agreeing to quarterly hearings before its Monetary Affairs Sub-Committee and to the presentation of the Bank's annual report before its plenary session. But despite much hype, these arrangements can scarcely be held to amount to accountability. Mr Duisenberg's idea appears to be that he will use the hearings and the annual report before the European Parliament as additional opportunities to those afforded by regular press conferences following ECB meetings for explaining the Bank's monetary policy to the European public. In other words, the European Parliament is perceived as a convenient platform, among others.

The Randzio-Plath report

MEPs will not be able to bring any direct influence to bear upon ECB decisions. For example, Mr Duisenberg squashed suggestions from the Chair of the Monetary Affairs Sub-Committee, Christa Randzio-Plath, ahead of her June 1998 report on ECB accountability, that members should receive privileged, confidential information regarding the Bank's deliberations and in particular, on its principal operating parameter, the definition of price stability. The European Parliament's capacity to assert itself in these circumstances is shackled by the lack of resources available to the Monetary Affairs Sub-Committee to secure expert advice, although its membership, which includes two former finance ministers and one former central bank governor, as well as several former bankers and currency traders compares favourably with its equivalent in most national legislatures. But, above all, the Parliament suffers from the generally low public esteem in which it is held and the absence of a genuinely European, as opposed to national, public opinion which it can influence and galvanise against the ECB.

Of course, these limitations have not prevented the Parliament increasing its powers in the past. And attempts have been made, primarily by Alan Donnelly in his amendments to the Randzio-Plath report, to give MEPs a vote of censure procedure for the President and Board, to require the formal approval of the European Parliament to the ECB's definition of price stability, and to insist that the ECB should simply report to the Parliament the impact of its monetary policy on unemployment levels. But these efforts have conspicuously failed to find support, even among colleagues — perhaps because of widespread resentment of British inspired proposals for a project in which the UK is not presently taking part. More significant, however, was the fact that the vast majority of mainstream MEPs support ECB independence, or, at least, have no desire to challenge, at this stage, the spirit, let alone the letter, of the Maastricht Treaty. The apparent acquiescence of MEPs in the ECB arrangements follows a well established pattern of European Parliamentary votes on meetings of the European Council, where those belonging to parties currently in government tend to follow instructions from back home. Indeed, the only MEPs to share British Socialist concerns over independent central banking seem to be the French Socialists and Gaullists, but they have been restrained by their general hostility to increasing the power of the European Parliament, and prefer to put their trust in the counterbalance of the Council of the Euro Eleven.

The role of ministers

On the face of it, the Council of the Eleven is the place to look for democratic control over the ECB. If democracy in Europe is likely to remain more national than European, then member state governments, operating together, are the true source of legitimate authority. Under the Maastricht Treaty the finance ministers retain responsibility for the Euro's exchange rate. They also control all of their respective official reserves over and above the relatively modest percentages directly allocated to the ECB, although substantial transactions in these will need, under the ECB Statute, the prior approval of the Governing Council. Above all, the ministers will be clearly responsible for fiscal and supply side policy coordination. Surely all this will prove a sufficient actual restraint by elected governments upon the 'unelected bankers' at the ECB, just as the Bundesbank and the US Fed are balanced by the fiscal and supply side policy powers of their respective executives and legislatures?

Although the single market requires some limited and specific increases in fiscal and supply side policy coordination, EMU will have a dramatic and immediate effect on the need for national and perhaps regional fiscal and supply side policy differentiation. The single monetary policy will lead to varying economic responses in individual countries and their regions. Without their own monetary policy, member states will be forced into greater fiscal and supply side policy activism. Paradoxically, this will increase the influence of national parliaments over the economy generally, because their powers over fiscal and supply side policy are clearly real, whereas their powers over monetary policy have been, where they have existed at all, largely formal.

The ECB, however, will be one institution running monetary policy sitting opposite not one government but at least eleven, each with its own fiscal and supply side policy. The Bank will have the opportunity for playing off one government against another if faced with no combined bargaining position.

Lasting independence

Whether or not such ECB independence can last will depend upon how the existence of the euro effects public perception. EMU is not just one of the greatest steps forward in European integration, it is also by far the most obvious. With Europe, literally, in one's pocket, feelings about the significance of European as opposed to national decision taking are bound to be transformed. Rather than compensating for different economic responses in individual countries through different fiscal and supply side policies, might not a sufficient sense of European solidarity develop to sustain a European government which addresses such inevitable inequalities through redistribution, allied to all out fiscal and supply side harmonisation? And might not the European Parliament become the principle focus for democratic representation, at least for questions of

European-wide economic management, developing the power to mobilise public opinion in order to challenge the ECB?

Perhaps. But even if this extremely remote prospect were to come about, it would not, necessarily, undermine the independence of the ECB which is at the heart of EMU. The Maastricht Treaty represents the triumph of the neo-liberal orthodoxy of de-politicised monetary policy. EMU is founded on the notion that the value of the currency is not one economic policy instrument among many to be manipulated at will, but rather is fundamental to the market system and therefore should be held stable, at least internally (or in other words, without inflation). Independent central banking — entrenching sound money — is thus as important to society as an independent system of justice is to enforcing property rights and contractual obligations, or an independent competition authority is to the functioning of a market economy. The constraints that independent central banks impose on the short-termism and sectionalism inherent in democratic processes is justified on the grounds that this constitutes the surest safeguard of individual wealth and collective wealth creation over the long term. It is the application to monetary policy of the general liberal notion that freedom and democracy, though related, are far from being synonymous.

Britain, the original home of these tenets, still, sadly, seems a long way from embracing them. Bizarrely, the anti-European right has become the passionate champion of political control over the Bank of England, whilst the incoming Labour government has granted it independence, albeit of a limited and flawed kind. Indeed, it has been the predominance of politicians for whom such a retreat from politics is fundamentally unwelcome which has done more than anything else to distort the EMU debate away from the rather mundane realities of running a multinational monetary regime. For the victory of independent central banking on the continent, though obviously owing much to the successful neo-liberalism of German post-war reconstruction, of which the Bundesbank has been the supreme expression, also rests on the necessity of de-politicising issues inherent in the general process of European integration.

One way to look at the deep unease felt by all governments, including the French, over the way the May 1998 summit exposed national horse trading, or at Mr Duisenberg's absolute insistence that the minutes of ECB meetings should not run any risk whatever of revealing how individual Board or Council members voted, is that lack of ECB accountability is recognised as essential to avoid any particular state seeking to pressurise or high-jack a monetary policy which must plainly be set for the euro zone as a whole. EMU is an historically unique exercise and requires safeguards and disciplines of a completely different order to those necessary within a single country. The European Central Bank is merely a super charged version of the principles of the rule of law and supranationality that underpin the status of the Commission. Just as the Commission is the guardian of the European treaties, so the European Central Bank is the guardian of the European single currency.

Of course, none of this might prove to be much of a guide to determining whether the ECB will be considered, over the medium term, as legitimate by the citizens of Euroland. The Commission may be unpopular, but it is not actually regarded as illegitimate, except by a minority even of the anti-Europeans. It is true that notions of independent central banking, whilst enjoying widespread support in Germany, the Netherlands and Austria, are still novelties in the political and economic culture of the remaining EMU participating states. On the other hand, these are also the countries most affected by ageing populations and a rapid growth of private pension provision. Such demographic and capital market trends are sometimes seen as obstacles to a successful EMU. In fact, an increasing number of retired people dependent on accumulated savings is almost tailor made to provide the political support necessary to sustain the sound monetary policy of which independent central banking is the most reliable guarantor.

Ultimately, the status of the ECB and the present Maastricht dispensation of independent central banking will depend upon the success of the euro and of the economy of the participating member states, as well as upon how that relates to general attitudes towards neo-liberal as opposed to more interventionist models of monetary management. That is very difficult to predict. What is certain, however, is that those who imagine that EMU will fail for a lack of democracy and legitimacy are utterly mistaken.

11. Superstate Euroland?

Andrew Duff

That Economic and Monetary Union might turn the European Union into a centralised superstate is a widespread fear. Some, doubtless, would welcome the emergence of a United States of Europe as a world power to rival the USA. Others would revolt against it. Most — including this author — would wish to avoid it, and would be prejudiced against the single currency if they thought such an over-centralisation of power were an inevitable consequence of its introduction.

In this chapter we look at how EMU will be run, by whom, and from where. Who calls the shots in the euro regime? Is the transfer of monetary sovereignty to EU institutions sustainable without the creation of a formal economic government? Does one European money mean one centralised European economy? Or is the euro merely a common medium of transaction for an economic area whose characteristics are diversity, decentralisation and, even, differentiation?

We favour the latter approach, and believe that the legal and political framework of EMU optimises conditions for Europe's enterprises. EMU equips Europe with the capability to respond to the demands of globalisation. The structural reform which it fosters, involving deregulation and the growth of the private sector, will encourage competitiveness, consolidate the single market and help the development of small and medium size companies. Only in conditions of deep-seated recession and external shocks might it be necessary to take refuge in 'big government', as the USA did in the 1930s after the Slump.

HOW EMU IS GOVERNED

How EMU will be governed was largely established by the Treaty of Maastricht, which the governments agreed to in December 1991. 'Member States shall regard their economic policies as a matter of common concern and shall coordinate them within the Council'.[1] The Council (of ministers of finance) — Ecofin — will monitor the performance of the domestic economic policies of each member state and publish their opinion. Where a member state breaches commonly agreed economic policy guidelines, or where the sustainability of the monetary union is jeopardised, the Council may articulate and publish recommendations addressed to the errant member state.[2] The intent of these procedures is that the Union's macroeconomic policy will be run collectively by the finance ministers in their Council. The use of qualified majority voting throughout implies that a significant element of mutual trust will permeate the proceedings, rather like a national cabinet.

Unanimity is reserved for bailing out a member state government in a crisis not entirely of its own making — 'severe difficulties caused by exceptional occurrences beyond its control'.[3] Otherwise overdrafts are not allowed, and the government of a profligate member state will have to accept the prospect of ruin. Governments who allow an excessive budgetary deficit to continue may be penalised by the Union. A member state failing to comply with the Council's instructions, formulated again by QMV, will face one or more of the following measures:

• be required to publish specific additional information before issuing bonds and securities;

• have its EIB loans frozen;

• be required to make an additional non-interest bearing deposit with the ECB;

• pay a fine 'of an appropriate size'.[4]

Although Ecofin will have the final say in coordinating the economic policies of the member states and in running the Union's own economic policy, the European Commission has a central role in gathering and analysing information, in negotiating changes to policy, in making proposals to the Council and in over-seeing the implementation of policy. And monetary policy, run by the European Central Bank, obviously impinges on economic policy. But at the end of the day, it is the member states which decide.

Putting theory into practice

Once the Maastricht Treaty had come into force in November 1993, the member states began to put flesh on what was still a skeletal frame for the supranational management of an economic policy. This process involved legal, technical and institutional preparations for making the transition to the euro. But it has also involved a reinforcement of the political will behind EMU and a consolidation of the mutual confidence with which ministers, their officials, the ECB and the Commission eye one another across the Council table.

Motivated at first by the need to establish methods of managing the relationship between the core members of Euroland on the one hand and the 'pre-ins' and 'outs' on the other, it soon dawned on everyone concerned that, for political and circumstantial reasons, it was going to be impossible to exclude from those joining in the first round in January 1999 certain member states — notably, Italy — which lacked long-term credibility in terms of budgetary discipline. Something therefore had to be done to strengthen the ties that bound the members of Euroland together if the ever-sceptical markets were to be reassured that EMU would work. If the euro core could not be narrow, as the Germans, at least, had originally intended, it should nevertheless be solid. One central banker even suggested, one supposes jocularly, that the no bail-out rule should be printed on all the euro notes.

Symbolic of this necessary, enhanced level of integration is the Stability and Growth Pact, negotiated at the Dublin European Council in December 1996 and promulgated at Amsterdam in June 1997. The Pact confirmed that member states 'remain responsible for their national budgetary policies' but spelled out the major constraints imposed by EMU on the autonomy of national governments.[5] National policy must be designed to support the stability-oriented monetary policy of the Union; member states commit themselves to maintaining fiscal policies that result in a balanced or surplus budget over the medium term; and both the Commission and Council are enjoined to act quickly and forcefully to correct deficit situations in any member state. To the multilateral surveillance of the economies of the member states is now to be added an overall assessment of the economic evolution of the EU as a whole. The Pact reasserts the freedom of assessment and judgement of the Commission and Council, and sets out the precise terms of the levies to be imposed on member states with deficits of more than 3% of GDP.

As a palliative to all this fiscal rigour, the Union leaders at Amsterdam, encouraged by recent electoral defeats for the right in Britain and France, tried to boost the salience of employment policy at the European Union level. 'That was not mere chance', says Commissioner de Silguy. 'It is clear that sound macroeconomic and fiscal policies go hand in hand with strong, job creating growth. The Pact will ensure permanently low interest rates that are conducive to investment, growth and, therefore, employment'.[6]

Jobs, however, will not flow ineluctably from EMU unless the European economy meets the challenge of globalisation by creating more flexible labour markets, improving its education and training, boosting its research and development, and enforcing competition policy. Whatever the rhetorical commitment of the European Council to employment (and it is great), jobs are provided, mostly, by business, while government is responsible only for the structural conditions within which business works. How the Union deals in practice with the issues of structural reform is variable, and the contribution of economic government at the EU level to microeconomic policy is strictly limited. As Iain Begg observes, the EU budget itself is presently too small, at about 3% of total public expenditure, to have more than a small impact on regional development, trans-European networking or R&D. The EU has only a marginal effect on up-grading the skills and education of the European workforce. The Commission is, of course, a very much more significant player in the field of state aids and competition policy, and there must be the strong possibility that the European Union — or at least certain of its member states — will at some stage not wish to resist the temptation of expanding its role into the other, sectoral areas of the integrating economy and its social dimension.

After all, the policy objectives of the Union go way beyond the creation of the single market and money. The EU and its member states are enjoined by the Treaty to adopt an 'economic policy which is based on the close coordination of Member States' economic policies, on the internal market and on the definition of common objectives, and conducted in accordance with the principle of an open market economy with free competition'.[7] The objectives are comprehensively (if inelegantly) spelled out as being:

> 'to promote throughout the Community a harmonious, balanced
> and sustainable development of economic activities, a high level
> of employment and of social protection, equality between men and
> women, sustainable and non-inflationary growth, a high degree of
> competitiveness and convergence of economic performance, a
> high level of protection and improvement of the quality of the
> environment, the raising of the standard of living and quality of
> life, and economic and social cohesion and solidarity among
> Member States'.[8]

It remains a matter of frustration, as evinced by John Monks, that the ambitious objectives of the December 1993 White Paper of the

Delors Commission on growth, competitiveness and employment, remain largely unfulfilled. This was a comprehensive package of analysis and proposals for a new model of sustainable development and 'active solidarity'.[9] It proposed a catalogue of measures to advance the use of information technology, to upgrade education and training, to build Trans-European Networks, to tax pollution, to facilitate labour market flexibility and to raise the level of capital investment, including direct EU investment. The White Paper's reception was marred by its coincidence with the depth of the recession and the fraught ratification process of the Maastricht Treaty, and it made little headway. But once EMU is established, the EU institutions will have a new opportunity to return to that agenda, and to reassess the Union's role in generating growth and competitiveness. It is not to be excluded that a future Ecofin may be willing to adopt a more *dirigiste* approach to economic policy. Indeed, one of the attractions of Euroland is that economic policy options widen.

Who runs monetary policy?

No uncertainty shrouds the future of the Union's single monetary policy. The European System of Central Banks is in charge. Its primary objective is to maintain price stability while supporting the general economic policies and objectives of the Union. Its principal tasks are:

- to define and implement the monetary policy of the Union;

- to carry out foreign exchange operations;

- to manage the official reserves of the Union;

- to promote the smooth operation of the payment systems.

The ESCB comprises the central banks of the member states plus the European Central Bank. The ESCB is run by a Governing Council made up of the governors of the national central banks of the euro countries and an Executive Board. The Board, which to all intents and purposes runs the show, comprises a president, vice-president and four members appointed, ostensibly, for an eight-year term. The Executive Board will implement monetary policy, and service and preside over the meetings of the Governing Council. Voting in the Governing Council will be qualified pro rata to a member state's reserve holding with the ECB. (The Bank's initial holding of foreign reserve assets amounts to almost euro 40 bn.) The Board (of six) will be out-numbered on the

Governing Council by the (initially, eleven) national governors, but by dint of its independence, coherence and quality of membership may be expected to dominate the proceedings. Besides, the 'national' central bank governors from the euro countries will have become, in effect, managers of the regional subsidiaries of the ECB, and will be strictly forbidden from taking instruction from their national treasuries.

The ECB can make binding regulations and decisions and non-binding recommendations and opinions. It will be consulted officially in numerous ways, and may, with the Commission, be involved in negotiations on behalf of the Union in relevant international affairs, such as the IMF.[10] Its relationship with the Commission promises to be a key determinant of its political role. Many duties are exercised by the ECB in parallel with the Commission, and it would clearly weaken the credibility of EMU were there to be a falling out between the two institutions on major matters of policy.

Both the Bank and the Commission have two representatives on an Economic and Financial Committee, along with two nominations each from every member state (it is presumed, one from the national treasury and the other from the central bank). This Economic and Financial Committee, which will replace the existing Monetary Committee, will prepare the meetings of Ecofin and oversee the running of the payments system. Its significance is that it provides Ecofin with an alternative source of specialist advice at the official level to that of Coreper. The permanent representatives of the member states in Brussels who sit in Coreper are traditionally beholden to the foreign ministries, and have had a powerful role to play in coordinating and brokering the multifaceted affairs of the Council. Ecofin will not be beholden to the same discipline, which may store up problems of internal government coherence, especially in external relations, in the years ahead.

Enhanced cooperation

The future role of Ecofin quickly fell under the spotlight when the British Chancellor of the Exchequer made a fuss about his exclusion from informal gatherings of his colleagues from Euroland. Quite why Gordon Brown should have presumed on his participation in a club to which he did not belong is too strange to relate. The Treaties of Maastricht and Amsterdam are quite explicit both about the need for and the design of a two-tier approach to EMU; there was always going to be specific differentiation between those who adopt the single currency and those who choose not to or cannot yet.

The British quarrel, which particularly annoyed the French, was resolved by affirming the 'defining position of the Ecofin Council at the centre of the economic coordination and decision-making process' of an economic and monetary union that involves all member states regardless of whether they have adopted the single currency.[11] But Mr Brown lost the particular argument, and the first so-called Euro Council of the Eleven took place during the official UK presidency of the Council with Rudolf Edlinger, the Austrian finance minister, in the chair (while Mr Brown headed for the airport).

The Council of the Eleven is set to become a regular feature of the system of governance of EMU. Representatives of the ECB, the Economic and Financial Committee and the European Commission will participate in its meetings, which will usually be held for two hours or so before the formal meetings of Ecofin. The remit of the Council of the Eleven is to 'discuss issues connected with their shared specific responsibilities for the single currency' — which is broad enough to discuss anything at all, including the euro's exchange rate with other currencies (not excluding sterling) and preparations for G7 (or G2). Mr Edlinger said that at its first meeting, the Eleven had conducted themselves 'with intensity and clarity', which, he added, 'is not always the case in European bodies'.[12]

As should be obvious by now, despite the importance that is rightly attached to the careful formulations of the Treaty, the Union is dealing quite pragmatically with how to govern EMU. The Luxembourg European Council in December 1997, for example, laid great emphasis on the need for a 'continuous and fruitful dialogue' between Ecofin and the ECB. A particularly sensitive issue, in the light of the need to respect the independence of the ESCB, is the (non-voting) participation of the President-in-office of the Council in meetings of the Governing Council of the ECB. To date, it has been agreed that the Council president should 'report' to the ECB the views of Ecofin on the economic situation in the EU and in the member states, and 'discuss' with the ECB the views of Ecofin on the exchange rate.[13] Assuredly, the ECB President will return the compliment by attending meetings of Ecofin.

The fact that EMU has created a multi-tiered European Union of the 'ins', 'pre-ins' and 'outs' is to be illustrated most starkly over the question of the representation of Euroland overseas. This cannot be left to the presidency of Ecofin because he or she will from time to time be a national from a non-euro state (the first will be a Swede in January 2001). The options include instituting a troika system of the previous, present and future Ecofin presidents, creating a directorate of the presidencies of Ecofin, the Commission and the ECB, or, even, appointing a 'M. ou Mme Euro' along the lines of the EU's new arrangement for common foreign and security policy.

Locating economic government

It is fairly obvious that what we have at the outset of the third stage of EMU does not amount to a European economic government. To date, after all, most attention has been paid to the running of a single monetary, rather than an economic, policy. Yet as the day of reckoning comes closer, the importance of getting the economics of EMU right grows fast. The main problem, clearly, is to coordinate budgetary policies when they are decentralised within one, centralised, and fairly rigid, monetary regime.

Whereas the Stability and Growth Pact provides the framework for a tighter budgetary regime for the member states, the overall budgetary position of Euroland is not so clearly constrained. Further coordination of budgetary policy would certainly be needed in the unlikely circumstances that, while individual member states conformed to the Stability Pact, the economic performance of the euro countries as a whole were to result in a balance of payments deficit.

The Stability Pact assumes that national governments are and will remain more or less in control of events in their member states. As we have seen in Italy, where the *tangentopoli* crisis has exposed the weakness of the state, this may be wishful thinking. A more extreme example of how monetary union could lead to political union may be imagined where one country was unable for domestic political reasons to take the necessary steps to correct an excessive deficit situation. In collusion with Ecofin (acting unanimously) and the ECB, the Commission might have no alternative but to assume some of the financial responsibilities of the defaulting member state. In such critical circumstances, at least a temporary centralisation of fiscal policy on Brussels would be inevitable — as well as welcome, presumably, to a majority of the citizens of the offending state.

Even in calmer times, and regardless of the Treaty-based independence guarantee of the ECB, which is particularly precious to the Germans, monetary and economic issues cannot easily be disengaged in the minds of the politicians who make up the Council or the European Parliament. Interest rate decisions of the ECB will have a direct, even dramatic impact on employment. How regions react will differ widely. In the new competitive regime of the euro, some service and product areas will be winners and some losers. Some regions will have the capability to assert themselves; others will be less successful.

The situation, at least for Euroland countries, will be dynamic. Economic convergence among the 'ins' is likely to increase. Corporate and savings taxation, for example, can hardly be left entirely to national choice and free competition, and some element of harmonisation will almost certainly be necessary. Although it will not disappear, the width of discretion over domestic taxation policy is likely therefore to narrow. Moreover, as the role of the euro as a global currency rapidly evolves, the European Union must acquire a sound and efficient mechanism for speaking with one voice on world monetary affairs.

In these circumstances, it must be doubted that informal collaboration in the ad hoc Council of the Eleven will prove to be tight enough. If the UK were to join EMU, along with Denmark and Sweden, and the only 'outs' were the poorer states from Central Europe, there would be every sense in up-grading Ecofin itself and in introducing to it a formal, two-tier structure. The so-called flexibility clauses of the Treaty of Amsterdam, which will come into force during 1999, provide the wherewithal for the formation of reinforced cooperation between the euro core within Ecofin itself.[14] For all concerned this would be a preferable outcome to the essentially transitory expedient — de Silguy warns of 'institutional digression' — of the informal Council of the Eleven.[15]

Given time, and such legitimate and practicable developments, it is likely that Ecofin would begin to be regarded, and to regard itself, as a super ministry of finance of the European Union presiding over a decentralised nexus of regional economies.

A federal central bank is born

During the May Day weekend, 1998, in Brussels, EMU enjoyed a rite of passage. Dominating world headlines, and suffocating the good news about the successful choice of the first eleven member states to enter the euro, was the fierce row (under the hapless British presidency) between France and Germany about the choice of the Dutch President of the European Central Bank. There is no doubt that, while it was perfectly proper for him to object to Wim Duisenberg's automatic transfer from the presidency of the EMI to that of the ECB, President Chirac's insistence on the appointment of a French national broke the spirit and the letter of the Treaty. It remains to be seen whether Mr Duisenberg's resulting equivocation over the length of his term leads to his early retirement or not. (In our view, it should not.)

But the real significance of the crisis over the May Day weekend is, first, that the job of President of the European Central Bank was suddenly and dramatically politicised, and, second, that the financial markets were unfazed by the whole thing. In fact, that the project could survive such a traumatic weekend involving a rupture between the twin godparents of EMU was a sign of its genuine robustness.

The ECB, as everyone knows, is modelled on the German Bundesbank. So it is important, in trying to gauge the character of the ECB, to understand that the Bundesbank, although independent of government, is not a sterilised technocratic body of bankers. It is a federal bank, with sinews that run from its office in Frankfurt deep into the heart of the German provincial economy. Nominally secret, its meetings, in the words of one central banker, 'leak like a sieve'. Especially since unification in 1990, the Bundesbank has had to cope with an economic recession, high unemployment and a huge diversity of economic performance between the Länder. To accomplish its overriding objective of price stability, the Bundesbank acts almost as if it were one of the nation's social partners, consulting others and informing itself about business and political trends and needs. The Bundesbank still remains, by all accounts, the most popular of German institutions.

The European Central Bank will not be able to achieve such credibility within European Union business circles, let alone such popular legitimacy, in a hurry. But there is no self-evident reason why it may not be able to emulate the Bundesbank in these respects given time and the right leadership.

One of the key issues is openness. To date, unfortunately, the ECB seems to be trying to establish rules of procedure that are antipathetic to the spirit of open government. Its minutes, apparently, will not be published for many years, and its voting records will be confidential. So there is more than a danger that public and parliamentary scrutiny of the performance of the ECB will be informed by leaks, anecdotes and speculation. We strongly agree with Willem Buiter, who argues:

'The ECB will have to learn that independence, far from being inconsistent with openness and accountability, cannot, in a democratic society, survive without these two awkward customers. The ECB is the latest offshoot of a central banking tradition that views central banking as a sacred, quasi-mystical vocation, a cult whose priests perform the holy sacraments far from the preying eyes of the non-initiates. This mystique of the central bank, and the excessive clubbishness and clannish behaviour it sometimes encourages, is both entirely unwarranted and a threat to the legitimacy of the purposes the central bank is intended to serve: price stability, preventing and coping with systemic financial risk and minimising the output and employment gaps'.[16]

A practical man, Mr Duisenberg already acknowledges the strength of the argument for more openness. He wants the monetary policy of the ESCB to be 'as transparent as possible'. The monetary authorities should 'make clear in word and deed' how they view the situation to the public and to politicians. This means publishing inflation targets and explaining deviations in order to achieve two precious qualities of good monetary policy, predictability and consistency. But the first President of the ECB still has to hit upon the right mix of discretion and transparency — as he says, 'not to throw the baby of independence out with the bathwater of accountability'.[17] Wim Duisenberg should be less coy. He and his colleagues in Eurotower, Frankfurt, would be wise to concede the prompt publication of the formal voting records as well as (non-attributory) minutes of the ECB and the Governing Council of the ESCB.

POLITICAL IMPLICATIONS OF EMU

This book has established beyond demur that economic and monetary union will have a profound effect on the future politics of the European Union as a whole. Whether or not Euroland will end up as a superstate depends. To summarise: an EMU which is popular and successful will feature the strong federative characteristics of diversity, democracy and decentralisation; a less successful EMU is likely to become more centralised politically, and more interventionist in terms of economic policy.

The Treaty and the steps taken to build on its framework as part of the preparation of the introduction of the single currency, postulate a successful EMU whose system of governance is akin to that of the European Union as a whole. EMU, in other words, is designed to cater for and treat with the same balance of power dynamics that have been developed across a wider field over the last half century. The question of balance has always been essential to the vitality of the Community system: between the institutions, between large and small member states, between the common and the national interest. EMU complicates the maintenance of equilibrium because it adds into the equation a new powerful institution, the ECB, and, in formalising multi-tier membership of the Union, it adds a new balancing act, that of the 'ins' and the 'outs'. But EMU is an extension of an existing and well-tried system of governance rather than a revolution in government itself.

Ingenuity will certainly be needed to run the single currency regime, but the European Union system is nothing if not ingenious. Scrupulous application of the twin principles of proportionality and subsidiarity will be more than ever necessary if the euro regime is not to adopt a bossy and fussy government. Proportionality means that the severity of the Union's actions should be related to the gravity of the problem they seek to address. Subsidiarity means that no decision or law should be taken by a higher authority when it can as effectively and efficiently be taken lower down. The wide diversity of economic conditions within Euroland suggests that not only will differentiation, for example, in employment policy be required, but that the principles of proportionality and subsidiarity will have to applied flexibly too. In other words, what is an appropriate delegation of authority to a Land government in Germany may be entirely inappropriate a degree of devolution for a regional council in France.

To sustain economic convergence, tough decisions will be needed by member state governments both individually and collectively, and the temptation will be, as always, to deflect national political pressure by blaming the European Union. A systematic policy of openness by the ECB, to which we have already referred, is its surest line of defence. But EMU also needs the protection — indeed, the advocacy — of a political class which will not dissemble about the scale and scope of European integration.

Politics at the federal level will have to be prepared to challenge and deflate those national politicians who seek to pass the buck to Frankfurt and Brussels. Politics at the national level will have to become less pretentious. EMU means that national politicians should no longer be able to enter an election campaign making absurd claims about their unilateral capabilities in the management of the economy. Domestic tax and spend pledges will make sense only in so far as they conform to the fiscal stance approved for each member state by Ecofin. A change of macroeconomic policy will only be accomplished in coordination with other member states and the institutions of the European Union. In the euro regime, persuasion will be valued more highly than braggadocio.

The need for more reform

As the new realities of EMU gradually impinge themselves upon the political consciousness of the member states and public opinion, transnational politics will surely develop. The democratic legitimisation of the euro is bound to galvanise those, for example, who advocate the evolution of truly European political parties, with common agendas, membership and leadership. In these circumstances, the European Parliament might soon become the dominant political forum of the European space with a single market and money. MEPs have already established a foothold in the scrutiny of appointments to the ECB, and have initiated a dialogue with its directors which could and should be supplemented by regular liaison with the Council's Economic and Financial Committee. The Parliament is already becoming comparable to the US Congress in that it is now the target of powerful European-level business lobbyists, trade union interests and NGOs, who effectively by-pass the national scene. The increasing respectability and responsibility of the European Parliament is illustrated in its own efforts to reform its electoral procedure so as to allow a portion of MEPs to be elected from transnational lists. It is to be hoped that the Parliament's growing maturity may also be reflected by an increased turnout in the June 1999 elections.

As the previous chapter has suggested, the European Parliament is unlikely to have a clear run at EMU. National parliaments will try to be involved, even if vainly. So will the European Union's consultative Economic and Social Committee and the Committee of the Regions — the former in any event desperate for a serious role, and the latter spurred by enhanced competition between the regions of Euroland. Graham Bishop is right to remind us of how thrusting autonomous regions will be competing against each other for the spread of credit. What this will do for inter-regional relations, and how subnational governments will organise themselves to best articulate their views individually and collectively at the EU level, remains to be seen. But the European Union institutions would be wise to cooperate and encourage.

The EU should also galvanise a new form of economic and social dialogue dedicated to EMU, either by adapting the existing (and woolly) tripartite discussions between the Commission, employers and trade union representatives, or by creating afresh an economic and social council of Euroland. Such an innovation may provide the perfect interlocutor for the Executive Board of the ECB, as well as spawning the emergence of truly transnational organisations to represent the interests of business and the workforce.

The important task of legitimising EMU in democratic terms, however, should not be allowed to be borne only by the European Central Bank, the Parliament and new or untried forms of economic and social partnership. Monetary union reinforces the argument for deepening the democratic accountability and effectiveness of all the European Union's institutions, and not least the Council. We have already seen how Ecofin might acquire, over time, the status of an EU ministry of finance. Such a development will not be reassuring either to the financial markets or to public opinion unless ministers and officials adopt the culture of openness. More transparency in the affairs of the Council is badly needed across the board, especially when they are acting in their legislative capacity. The European media also have a responsibility to help make the politics of Brussels more accessible.

A key element in the development of the Council is an extension of QMV, plus co-decision with the Parliament, to cover all law-making in the field of the single market and its flanking policies (except, probably, taxation). And in order to formulate and implement policy more efficiently, both the European Commission and the Council need a significant measure of internal reform. These changes, and others, are postulated by the self-evident incompleteness of what has been achieved by the Treaties of Maastricht and Amsterdam. A new intergovernmental conference (IGC) is presaged to coincide, somewhat incongruously, with the soon anticipated enlargement of the Union. The impact of the euro coupled with enlargement compounds the importance and urgency of institutional change within the Union. The new IGC should surely have the courage to reappraise in the light of experience the EMU chapter of Maastricht (untouched by Amsterdam), as well as to examine afresh the sub-treaty acquis, notably the Stability Pact.

The European Council of heads of state or government should not be allowed to escape reform. At present, it is not well-prepared to play its part in the legitimisation of the single currency and the good management of economic policy. The leaders have an unfortunate tendency to trip lightly around complex issues, and to issue solemn declarations which, when held up to analysis, turn out to be rather facile. Their growing involvement in the routine work of the Council is not always helpful to their ministerial colleagues or, for that matter, to the Commission or Parliament. The European Council has purloined the coordinating work of the General Affairs Council of foreign ministers, and only rarely contributed real added value in terms of forceful political direction. It is also a poor creature in a crisis: during the notorious May weekend in Brussels, the European Council was only one temper tantrum away from disaster. In short, the European Council must become consistently more trustful and trustworthy if it is to play a useful part in consolidating economic and monetary union. The public needs leadership on a European scale.

Understanding the euro

Economic and monetary union will not work well, of course, unless the European citizen becomes more actively engaged in the political economy of the new Europe. The introduction of the single currency is the high point of a process of European unification which is breaking down traditional power-based relationships between sovereign states and their disciplined peoples. Transcending national barriers is a new Treaty-based system of rules of fair play, procedures of check and balance, and agreed norms of behaviour. At the heart of this Europe lies a public which is starting to realise that neither economic livelihood nor political well-being is now confined or confirmed by the nation state. Price stability and transparency will be quickly established by EMU, and their popularity with consumers should lead in time to the creation of a new civic consensus around the euro.

There is no more dramatic symbol of the transition to a postnational Europe than the single currency now on offer. Economic and monetary union is not without its risks, and this book has been frank about them. But for all these risks there are contingencies, and the Treaty on European Union provides ample safeguards. The more we understand the euro, the less we need fear an ambush.

[1] Article 102a (**Article 98**).
[2] Article 103(4) (**Article 99(4)**).
[3] Article 103a(2) (**Article 100(2)**).
[4] Article 104c(11) (**Article 104(11)**).
[5] European Commission, *Stability and Growth Pact*, Bulletin of the European Union, 6/1997, p. 17.
[6] Yves Thibault de Silguy, AMUE Newsletter No. 24.
[7] Article 3a (**Article 4**).
[8] Article 2 (**Article 2**).
[9] European Commission White Paper, *Growth, Competitiveness, Employment: The challenges and ways forward into the 21st century*, EC Bulletin Supplement 6/93.
[10] As it stands, the statutes of the IMF allow only for the representation of states, so a period of assimilation, even confusion can be expected as the world community adjusts to the reality of the euro.
[11] European Commission, *Resolution of the European Council on Economic Policy Coordination in Stage Three of EMU and on Treaty Articles 109 and 109b*, Bulletin of the European Union, 12/1997, p. 18.
[12] Agence Europe, 6 June 1998.
[13] Ibid.
[14] Article 5a (**Article 11**).
[15] Agence Europe, 28 May 1998.
[16] *Britain and EMU*, Speech to the CEPR, London, 1 July 1998. Buiter is Professor of International Macroeconomics at the University of Cambridge and a member of the Monetary Policy Committee of the Bank of England.
[17] Seventh Bernard Mandeville Lecture, Rotterdam, 5 March 1998.